REDEFINING LEADERSHIP

COMPETING IN ASIA IN
THE 21ST CENTURY

REDEFINING LEADERSHIP

COMPETING IN ASIA IN THE 21ST CENTURY

GERRY DAVIS
AND
STEPHEN LANGTON

JOSSEY-BASS™
An Imprint of
WILEY

Copyright © 2009 by Gerry Davis and Stephen Langton. All rights reserved.

This edition is published by John Wiley & Sons (Asia) Pte. Ltd., 2 Clementi Loop, #02-01, Singapore 129809 on behalf of Jossey-Bass, A Wiley Imprint.

989 Market Street, San Francisco, CA 94103-1741–www.josseybass.com

No part of this publication may be reproduced, stored in a retrieval system, or transmitted in any form or by any means, electronic, mechanical, photocopying, recording, scanning, or otherwise, except as permitted under Section 107 or 108 of the 1976 United States Copyright Act, without either the prior written permission of the publisher, or authorization through payment of the appropriate per-copy fee to the Copyright Clearance Center, Inc., 222 Rosewood Drive, Danvers, MA 01923, 973-750-8400, fax 978-646-8600, or on the Web at www.copyright.com. Requests to the publisher for permission should be addressed to the Publisher, John Wiley & Sons (Asia) Pte. Ltd., 2 Clementi Loop #02-01, Singapore 129809, tel: 65-64632400, fax: 65-64646912, email: inquiry@wiley.com.

Readers should be aware that Internet Web sites offered as citations and/or sources for further information may have changed or disappeared between the time this was written and when it was read. Limit of Liability/Disclaimer of Warranty: While the publisher and author have used their best efforts in preparing this book, they make no representations or warranties with respect to the accuracy or completeness of the contents of this book and specifically disclaim any implied warranties of the merchantability or fitness for a particular purpose. No warranty may be created or extended by sales representatives or written sales materials. The advice and strategies contained herein may not be suitable for your situation. You should consult with a professional where appropriate.

Neither the publisher nor author shall be liable for any loss of profit or any other commercial damages, including but not limited to special, incidental, consequential, or other damages.

Jossey-Bass books and products are available through most bookstores. To contact Jossey-Bass directly call our Customer Care Department within the U.S. at 800-956-7739, outside the U.S. at 317-572-3986, or fax 317-572-4002.

Jossey-Bass also publishes its books in a variety of electronic formats. Some content that appears in print may not be available in electronic books.

Library of Congress Cataloging-in-Publication Data

ISBN: 978-0470-82435-1

Typeset in 10.5/13pt Sabon-Roman by Thomson Digital

Printed in Singapore Saik Wah Press Pte. Ltd.

10 9 8 7 6 5 4 3 2 1

CONTENTS

Acknowledgments — vii
About the Authors — ix
Foreword — xiii

    Introduction — 1

I Leading Yourself — 11

1. The Rise and Rise of Asia Pacific — 13
2. The Evolving C-Suite — 29
3. Getting to the Top: Leadership Development — 51

II Leading Others — 67

4. Building and Keeping Teams — 69
5. Executive Talent Management — 81
6. Mentoring, Coaching and Setting an Example — 97

III Leading the Future — 115

7. Enter the Dragon: China — 117
8. The Elephant in the Room: India — 133
9. The Future of Business Leadership in Asia Pacific — 147
10. Conclusion — 165

    Index — 189

ACKNOWLEDGMENTS

Just as no business leaders can succeed in a vacuum, no business authors can write a successful book alone. We could not have written this book without the help of our colleagues at Heidrick & Struggles Asia Pacific, whose knowledge and experience are filtered throughout these pages.

We would like to place on record the invaluable contributions of Alice Au, Alicia Yi, Arvind Mathur, Charles Moore, David Pumphrey, Fergus Kiel, Gary Dick, Gauri Padmanabhan, Jake Gordon-Clark, Jerome Bucher, Karen Choy-Xavier, Li-Ming Wen, Linda Zhang, Luis Moniz, Michael Thompson, Navnit Singh, Tony O'Leary, and Torbjorn Karlsson, who helped shape this book. We are especially grateful to Steve Mullinjer and Arun Shankar Das Mahapatra for their priceless inputs on China and India respectively.

Special thanks to Chief Marketing Officer Anna Yong who inspired and encouraged this project, and her Asia Pacific Marketing team including Thomas Liddle and Patricia Ooi who made this book possible.

Thanks also to Senior Publishing Editor C.J. Hwu at our publisher John Wiley & Sons (Asia), for lending her ideas, experience and editorial guidance.

Finally, we must thank the hundreds of executives and client corporations whose experience is represented here. Their trust in our expertise has been a two-way street: they have enlightened us, just as we have endeavored to enliven their careers and energize their companies.

ABOUT THE AUTHORS

Charles Gerry Davis
Managing Partner, Global Practices &
Regional Managing Partner, Asia Pacific
Heidrick & Struggles
Gerry is responsible for leading and shaping Heidrick & Struggles' client-facing activities and initiatives. He was previously regional managing partner, Asia Pacific, where he led the region through a period of unprecedented growth to assume clear market leadership. Earlier, Gerry led the CIO, Technology and Professional Services Practices in Asia Pacific.

Prior to joining Heidrick & Struggles, Gerry was the executive director of an international search firm conducting assignments for leading technology and professional services firms. Clients included both established corporations and start-up businesses.

Before entering the executive search industry, Gerry was managing director of On Australia Pty Ltd., a joint venture between Telstra and Microsoft to deliver Internet and online services. This business became Australia's largest Internet services provider and portal site. Prior to this, Gerry was CEO of one of Australia's largest software and services companies, Lend Lease Employer Systems. Later, he was the executive director for business development of Australasia's largest information services company, ISSC Australia (IBMGSA).

Gerry commenced his career as an officer in the Royal Australian Navy before joining PA Consulting, where he conducted assignments in logistics, operations, and organization development. He then joined AFP Group PLC, where he was responsible for evaluating and integrating acquired businesses in the United Kingdom and Australia.

Gerry then joined Booz, Allen and Hamilton in South East Asia, where he helped establish their Australian office, and led strategy and business process reengineering assignments.

Gerry Davis has a Bachelor of Arts in economics and a Master of Commerce in accounting and financial management from the University of New South Wales, a Graduate Diploma in finance from the University of Technology, Sydney, and a Master of Business Administration in strategy and management from the University of Washington.

Stephen Langton
Global Practice Managing Partner, Leadership Consulting
Heidrick & Struggles
Stephen has been privileged to provide assessment and development to the leaders of some of the world's leading organizations over the past 10 years. Having begun his career in executive search with Amrop International in Sydney in 1996, he made the transition from "poacher" to "gamekeeper" with the introduction of management audit services in the industry.

He has led major succession planning, management audit, and leadership development programs internationally for some of the region's largest organizations in the banking, paper, media, foods, technology, and entertainment industries. Within this, he has been responsible for the development of more than 20 CEOs and C-suite teams.

Stephen has been responsible for the delivery of such services across the Asia Pacific region for AT Kearney, and subsequently for TMP worldwide. He has most recently been director–Asia Pacific for Leading Initiatives Worldwide, where he led projects in China, Hong Kong, Korea, Singapore, India, and Japan. His clients have included market leaders such as Philips, Oracle, Commonwealth Bank, the ABC, Sony, Societe Generale, Merrill Lynch, News Corporation, and AMP.

His experience includes the worldwide evaluation of leaders in international restructuring projects, as well as some of the region's highest-profile corporate mergers. He has designed and led the "due diligence" of executives for capital investments, corporate restructuring, and acquisition selections. In addition, he has worked with a number of multibillion-dollar global corporations in designing processes for benchmarking talent in succession planning, developing and delivering leadership workshops, and preparing executives for shared services and cultural integrations.

Stephen technically qualified for this work by completing an MBA at the Australian Graduate School of Management. During this time, he studied under and consulted with acclaimed professors in this field. He has been a guest lecturer in leadership assessment and development on the MBA program at the Australian Graduate School as well as at Queensland University.

Prior to his career in business, Stephen served 10 years as an officer and pilot in the British Army. Commissioned at the Royal Military Academy, Sandhurst, in 1986, he saw service in numerous countries and appointments culminating in his acting command of the Army's leading armed-helicopter squadron engaged in United Nations duties.

About Heidrick & Struggles in Asia Pacific

Heidrick & Struggles is the world's premier provider of senior-level executive search and leadership consulting services, including talent management, board building, executive on-boarding, and M&A effectiveness. For more than 50 years, we have focused on quality service and built strong leadership teams through our relationships with clients and individuals worldwide. Since our first Asian office opened in 1989, Heidrick & Struggles has been working closely with Asian leaders from both the commercial and nonprofit sectors. Our consultants consistently demonstrate true passion in understanding all the nuances of our clients' needs, and have helped to identify, engage, and bring on board the best leaders for more than 350 of the world's leading companies operating in the region.

FOREWORD

I heard a colleague say something recently that I wish every senior executive—or would-be senior executive—had posted on the office wall:

"What counts the most are the things you learn *after* you think you know it all."

If you want to break through the "Peter Principle"—the observation that in a hierarchy, employees all tend to rise to their level of incompetence—this advice must be heeded. Yet how difficult it is. People rise through the ranks and, inevitably, hit a plateau. That plateau may be high, thanks to hard work and diligence, but moving onto the next level requires new muscles, untried paths, and dangerous ascents. No wonder many simply remain in middle management, casting only a wary eye toward peaks that seem tantalizingly close, yet beyond their reach.

Those who do continue the climb are answering the call of leadership. Anyone can lead a group through the foothills, but to get to the top requires a level of teamwork, collaboration, and perseverance that only true leaders can inspire. It's one thing to climb alone; it's another to recognize the skills of others and motivate them to reach new heights.

There is no greater risk or reward than leading a team across borders, which in the end is the greatest challenge for many would-be leaders. And never has the promise or peril been greater than for those corporations in the Asia Pacific region. In a way, we are talking about a fictional place, this *Asia*. How can the vast variety of markets, cultures, and know-how that stretches from Tokyo to Mumbai be summed up in one word? If I had to try, I would choose this word: *opportunity*.

Historically, the revenues for any multinational corporation are 50 percent to 70 percent from their home country. That is changing fast, thanks to the exploding markets of India, China, and the other developing economies in the region. As the financial crisis of 2008 has shown, economies are intertwined as never before. Companies now are heavily reliant on other countries and cultures to achieve their business objectives. The stakes couldn't be higher—companies that can't climb the summits of Asia will fall off the mountain.

This new era requires a new kind of corporate leader in the Asia Pacific market. That's where Heidrick & Struggles comes in. This book, the first of its kind, is a compendium of the thought leadership practice that has made our company the number one advisory firm for C-level executives in Asia. Our rise echoes the rise of the region—when we started our first office in Sydney in 1989, we were last among the top four executive recruitment firms in Asia. We are now on top, thanks to the values that make up the core of the advice we give our clients: acquiring the right talent, retaining existing talent, and grooming able leaders.

That success is built by the expertise of our employees, who take local understanding of specific industries and combine it with global benchmarks to create the deepest pool of insight into the leadership needs of companies in Asia. Whether it's life science in Singapore, private equity in Hong Kong, industrial management in China, or technology in India, we give the best advice based on our experience working with the best companies here and around the world. Our clients expect nothing less.

On a personal note, I'm passionate about the journey of corporations in the Asia Pacific market because it's been my journey, too. I first came to Asia from the United States as a wide-eyed Virginia boy with some experience in banking and a sense of adventure, taking a teaching job in Japan in my 20s. Little did I know then how wonderful that adventure would be, thanks to finding a career I became passionate about and working for a company that both encouraged and challenged me. My mentors at Heidrick & Struggles helped me climb out of my own "Peter Principle" plateau time and again.

My path toward the honor of becoming the company CEO started in Asia. My decade in Asia made me a better listener, more accepting of new and different ideas, and able to change my mind and admit mistakes—all crucial elements of continuing to learn after you think you know it all.

What is happening now in corporate leadership in Asia Pacific is on the cutting edge of a new era. The great business leaders of the 21st century are here. The challenge for any company now is to find them, nurture them, and get them on the mountain.

There is no shortage of peaks to climb in the Asian business world.

L. Kevin Kelly
Chief Executive Officer
Heidrick & Struggles International

INTRODUCTION

Innovative Leadership

In the best of times, good business leaders are in high demand. In bad times, great business leaders are crucial. This is a time for great business leaders, and Asia is where they must be found, deployed, and nurtured. The survival of any multinational firm—or companies that hope to become global concerns—depends on how well they do here. The events in the last half of 2008 have truly set the stage for greatness. The business world stood aghast as the subprime mortgage crisis ensnared Wall Street, bringing down some of the largest investment banks and triggering government bailouts of banking systems across the developed world. The financial fallout threw the United States, the world's largest economy, into recession, and the freefall in world stock markets generated headlines reminiscent of the Great Depression.

But many things have changed since the 1929 stock market crash triggered the global economic pain of the 1930s. Chief among the changes is the financial might of the Asia Pacific region. Japan laid the groundwork half a century ago, emerging from the ashes of World War II to become the second-largest economy in the world. In the past quarter century, China has moved from economic backwater toward the head of the table among nations, and it is on track to overtake the United States as the world's largest economy in the next one. India, which will pass China as the world's most populous nation in the same period, has a burgeoning economy led by intellectual outsourcing that has boosted the fortunes of both the country and the multinational companies that tap into its wealth of talent.

Even before the credit crisis, the Asia Pacific region was clearly pivotal for the future of any multinational company. Now corporate leaders eye the markets of India, China, and the rest of Asia like passengers on a leaky ship assessing the lifeboats. Any question that the region is a do-or-die market for survival is no longer academic. As the global financial capital markets contract, it is upon its vast human capital that the Asia Pacific region stands as a beacon to guide multinational corporations through the difficult waters ahead.

Time for Leadership Courage

Few Champagne corks fly from the balconies of corporate headquarters these days. Those privileged to celebrate a business success do so discreetly and with reverence, for times have changed. For too many years, we have told ourselves that the money would never run out, that we were more powerful and clever than the mass stupidity of our markets, that resource limitation was someone else's problem.

That myth ended. Time to work again. A box on the wall houses the word *Leadership*. On its front are the bold words: "In Case of Emergency, Break Glass."

Courage in leadership is about to come back into fashion. It marks the difference in leaders who will thrive in these uncertain times.

Courage is one of the very few words that we still use with careful reverence in our modern business world. So many others are abused and fraudulently used to imply the presence of a capability that does not exist or imply comparison of an environment to one that would be demanding enough to warrant them. We overuse the lexicon of human capability too often in the business world. Only a tiny few senior managers of businesses can really be observed as leaders, and the environment has to require leadership for that to be observed. No doubt the top echelons of businesses do include some strong strategic managers, but precious little happens in a business to demand or expect the true quality and capability of leadership—where people look to their superior for more than instructions—where they seek hope, belief, faith, and strength.

Arguably, operations at a mine, an oil platform, or other unpredictable environments of personal risk may become forums for the true demand and realization of leadership. But not the city. Few employees seek faith, strength, hope, and belief from their CEO or immediate manager. Crisis? What crisis? If a CEO makes a decision that collapses the market capitalization of a company overnight, every single one of its employees will still come in to work the next day...and go home safely at the end of it. When most people go home in the evening and come back again in the morning, little more is demanded of corporate leadership than the competence to tell them what they have to do, how it will be measured, and how they will be paid for it.

Until now. Until the predictability of the environment changes drastically. Until faithful employees are taken a rung down Maslow's hierarchy of human needs. Until our certainty of being able to afford the lives we have chosen decays and our beliefs about our security blur. When our national leaders speak out on economic crisis alongside words such as *survive*, *protect*, and *hope*, we know that elegant management alone will not see us through.

It is times such as these when, finally, leadership is critical. Indeed, as if illuminated by some collective awakening, it is only in such times when we can see so clearly whether we feel we are being well-led or not, and by whom. New leaders are revealed from those apparently competent managers who can adapt. Many so-called leaders are unmasked as frauds in their inability to communicate, calm, and rally the people who look to them. It is these times where leadership will determine a demoralized or an engaged workforce.

We have negligently forgotten this supreme competence. Most organizations have defined leadership capability lists that sound powerful but would be barely recognized as important in environments of real leadership need.

Commercial insight, developing talent, innovation and creativity, strategic thinking, customer insight, cooperation, change leader. These are merely implied tasks of the one competence of leadership. Used in the right context, it needs no further definition. It was a sign of the times that in the corporate world, we have had to define leadership in terms of values, principles and definitions. In environments that need leadership, the presence of it—or its absence—is absolutely clear to those around.

By the Book

During business downturns, sales of business self-help books spike. Dedicated followers of business fashion know the lexicon and follow the fads. Tomes by Peter Drucker and Warren Bennis lie under their pillows; they quote the words of former chairman Jack Welch of General Electric (GE) or uber-investor Warren Buffet with gospel-like solemnity. They speak acronym with the best of them: With their QMS, they keep close track of KPI to ensure TQM for best ROI. They are confident of their IQ and are working on their EQ (as perhaps demanded by HQ). (For the rest of the world, that's the quality management system they're using to track key performance indicators in pursuit of total quality management and return on investment. Confident of their traditional intelligence quotient, they're working on emotional intelligence, possibly at the behest of corporate headquarters.)

What is not on their lips can be easily found on their shelves. Want to add some spice to your career? Read *The Kama Sutra of Business*. Want to find your inner Buddha for your PowerPoints? How about some *Presentation Zen*? Can't find your fight in a rough-and-tumble market? Try *Sun Tzu: The Art of War for Managers* (or *The Art of War for Executives*. Or *Sun Tzu and the Art of Business*. Or . . .)

We mention the growing diversity of gurus, business help books, and management fads not to belittle them. We live in an age where the profusion of management and career advice is not only understandable—it is inevitable. With the loss of lifetime employment, things that used to happen naturally within a company—such as grooming future leaders, improving career skills, and mentoring—now have to be purpose-built within an organization. Executives hop from job to job and from industry to industry, building a portfolio career of their own design as they seek the best opportunities and the right fit. So if you think it will help, have a go at it: Get that black belt in Six Sigma. Walk over hot coals at a self-help seminar. Drum up office morale with a group bongo and conga session.

As executives at the premier leadership advisory firm in Asia however, we at Heidrick & Struggles Asia Pacific can't be mere followers of fashion. Nor can we claim a one-size-fits-all solution for the companies we advise—and the C-level executives we place at some of the largest corporations in the region. The industries and markets we serve are too diverse for a 10-point guide to finding the best leaders and building the best management team.

Yet we do see guiding principles that cut across countries, cultures, and businesses. We know we're on the right track because our business in Asia Pacific has tripled since the start of the new century as a result of putting these principles in practice for our clients. Our success mirrors the success of our clients. We must give the best leadership intelligence and advice, because our clients expect nothing less in the world's most dynamic market.

The Black Hole of Asia Business Leadership

The power of metaphor is undeniable when advising companies on best principles and practices in the hypercompetitive Asia Pacific market. For us, the most apt metaphor for business leadership comes not from texts of ancient spiritual manuals nor antique treatises on Chinese warfare, but from one of the elemental forces that drive the universe. When we walk into boardrooms around the region, we often start by asking company directors to do one simple exercise: draw a black hole.

It's a bit of a trick. As physics explains, black holes are objects in space whose gravitation is so dense that nothing—not even light—can escape. Therefore, the swirling shape of artist renderings, like water flowing down a drain, really only represent the way these powerhouses influence nearby stars and other matters. In other words, you can't draw a black hole. You can only draw how it impacts the objects around it.

Similarly, when we are asked to recruit new chief executives for our clients or evaluate a company's management, that is the yardstick by which we measure their leadership capabilities—their ability to attract and keep talented employees, produce world-class products and services, expand market share, and generate profits. In short, how they impact the company, its employees, and its shareholders.

Unfortunately, the black hole metaphor cuts both ways. Good business leaders in the Asia Pacific market are hard to find and in high demand. It's a seller's market for executive candidates who have both deep understanding of, say, the exploding domestic opportunities in China, and the broad ability to operate in the global environment that leading multinational firms demand. There's just not enough of this caliber of executives to go around.

Across the world, executives are under increased pressure to perform. CEO termination due to poor performance is up 70 percent compared to 10 years ago; the average tenure of CEOs is shrinking even as their average age comes down. More executives are retiring early, either by choice or by ouster; retirement age for CEOs is down to between 54 and 60 in Asia.

This creates a growing vacuum of able leaders to head multinational firms in Asia Pacific at a time when able leadership is most needed. The challenges and opportunities in exploding markets such as China and India can make or break firms today (and predict which companies will still be industry leaders tomorrow). The right leadership can steer companies toward unprecedented rewards. A wrong turn at the top, however, can cause a slip into oblivion, a lost opportunity that will never return.

Innovation Versus Fashion

Corporations and their executives must constantly look over one shoulder at competitors as they plot a course forward into the future. For the unseasoned executive or the growing corporation, this constant head-swiveling can create vertigo—uncertainty and a natural desire to latch onto the latest thing—lest they be left behind. It creates tension between what is truly innovative in leadership management and what will be considered passé a few years down the road. "Innovative leadership" is a buzzword in our industry, but the real test is the leaders who remain when the buzz is gone.

Our definition of innovative leadership is simple: A good CEO creates conditions for others to succeed.

But "simple" should not be confused with "easy." In sports, the adage is "play the game that got you there." But as one participant at a conference on business innovation we partnered in Tianjin, China, said: "Innovation should be focused on meeting market needs—current and emerging—and targeted at 'changing the game.'" To change the game in business, you must know the game—know your industry, know your skills, know best practices. But if you simply repeat what others do—or what you've done in the past—you can't change the game. Many executives plateau at a level of competence where they are simply recycling what they know, unaware that their playing style is for a game that has already been changed by others. Truly innovative leaders break new ground by seeing slightly ahead on the horizon of market needs and applying what they've learned in new ways to meet that need.

Innovative leaders are learners—their curiosity is keen. They are gifted communicators, not just in getting their message out, but also in taking in feedback from employees, clients, their board—really all stakeholders. They have a clear vision to guide their company beyond the horizon; they can correct their steering through the storms without losing sight of their goals.

These leaders stand out through the performance of their company and its employees. CEOs are required to be increasingly visible to shareholders, but getting noticed doesn't equal getting the job done, as Carly Fiorina discovered when she was CEO of Hewlett-Packard (HP). In a sense, great leaders are less "seen" by the general public and more "heard" by their ability to shepherd their company, attract and retain talented staff, and create value for customers as well as shareholders.

Following fashion can lead to disaster. What worked for Jack Welch at GE doesn't translate for all companies; in China, for example, letting go the bottom 10 percent performers (as was Welch's philosophy) wouldn't work because the turnover is so high and the demand so great. There, talent attraction and retention are crucial. A leader's management style must fit that company in that particular industry and market.

Elements of Leadership

We are living in an age where the practices most associated with innovation emerged with technology companies in North America. The pendulum historically swings both ways—it wasn't so long ago that best business practices in manufacturing were emerging from Japan, and the West was clamoring to catch up. The difficulty of *innovation* is it means different things in different contexts for different companies or industries. Innovators aren't just the people who are technically gifted at new products and design, new ways to deploy technology, or creating new technology itself. The most useful definition of innovation was given to us by post-World War II Japanese companies—the philosophy of *kaizen*, or constant improvement.

Innovative leadership isn't glamorous. It's head-down dedication, hard work and the ability to inspire the same in others. The new CEO of one of our clients, a leading food manufacturer in Australia, recently had to find another $3 million to turn the operation from red to black in one business quarter. Each time more funds were demanded, management saw the leadership responsibility as working even longer hours to seek more big-ticket items and units to harvest. This new CEO saw that this as a "management" response. The "leadership" response was far more successful: the company had 3,000 employees—if each employee could find $1,000 in savings or additional income, then the goal would be met. Not all staff members could find $1,000 to add to the company ledger, but no matter—some found as much as $14,000 (no doubt they would be remembered come the next round of reviews). The CEO met his goals, which were also the goals of his employees, so everyone owned the turnaround.

Innovative leaders learn, but how do they do that? By looking and listening, especially to their own employees. Understanding best practices of an industry is essential, but even more important is to understand your own company and employees, their strengths and weaknesses, the "points of pain" for the company. An innovative culture nurtures and stimulates employees to look for ways to improve what they do, no matter the industry, no matter the job. Innovative leaders have the ability to release the pent-up creative force within their organization, unleashing the desire within all to refine and improve what they do.

This book is intended for readers who want to understand the importance of people and interpersonal skills in driving business and career success. (And as any CEO would tell you, once you reach the top rung, managing people makes or breaks your job.) For those starting their career climb, this book is organized to help understand what it takes to get to the top job. We look at the rising importance of Asia, and how it will become the center of strategy for any multinational corporation—and any would-be executive—in the world. We look at how stalwart positions at the top of the company—such as the chief executive, financial, and operating officer (CEO, CFO, and COO)—are changing, and how new positions such as chief intelligence officer, chief marketing officer and chief human resources officer are bringing needed expertise into the boardroom.

For executives, we examine the skills needed to navigate the fast-changing business world of Asia Pacific. Be it cross-cultural difficulties, maintaining communication skills with home office and across the region, or solving disputes among employees, these are issues that all managers face as they move up the ladder, leaving tactical roles that emphasize technical skills and taking on strategic roles that call for people skills. We examine the importance of succession strategies, as well as important factors to attract and retain the best talent in markets where competition for employees is at a fevered pitch.

For the experienced executive, the book reveals insights into the markets and trends that will shape the future, such as the growing domestic and international economic might of China and India; the challenges of leading an organization with employees across multiple generations and a wide variety of skill sets; and the expanding leadership gap the world over—which must, inevitably, be filled by a new generation of global business leaders born in Asia.

Two elements you will see mentioned throughout this book are key for any successful career: building relationships and communication skills. These are skills that must be constantly nurtured and redefined, especially the higher one climbs up the corporate ladder. The ways one can be a good communicator and builder of networks are as varied as people themselves, but the results can be simply defined:

- Listening and sifting through many open streams of information—often from top-quality people who surround you—to make appropriate decisions.
- Effectively defining goals and providing support for subordinates to deploy your decisions.

Finally, the need for a multinational mind-set is crucial for companies and executives to succeed. Companies need globally minded employees and executives both at home and running their international operations. As international barriers to workforce mobility decline, the net to catch competent employees must be spread across national borders. Advice, analysis, and improvement of management practices for domestic and multinational executives will become a constant and continuous part of staying competitive in an increasingly borderless marketplace.

How to Use This Book

This book is the cumulative product of our thought leadership for some of the most important companies and executives in Asia Pacific. It's divided into three sections: Leading Yourself, Leading Others and Leading the Future.

> Part One: Leading Yourself
> Chapter 1: The Rise and Rise of Asia Pacific
> Chapter 2: The Evolving C-Suite
> Chapter 3: Getting to the Top: Leadership Development

To succeed in the Asia Pacific corporate world, you need to know the lay of the land. These chapters are focused on the importance of the region in the world of business, the positions in which company leaders are emerging, and the leadership skills that are most sought after.

> Part Two: Leading Others
> Chapter 4: Building and Keeping Teams
> Chapter 5: Executive Talent Management
> Chapter 6: Mentoring, Coaching and Setting an Example

In these chapters, we drill down into issues that are of top importance to companies today, such as attracting and keeping the best talent, helping them with skills that will both help them personally succeed in their careers and help company executives reach their goals.

Part Three   : Leading the Future
Chapter   7 : Enter the Dragon: China
Chapter   8 : The Elephant in the Room: India
Chapter   9 : The Future of Business Leadership in Asia Pacific
Chapter 10 : Conclusion

Here, we imagine the issues that are of particular importance in the two economies that will most decide the fate of corporate Asia in the coming decades: China and India. As the game continues to change in Asia, we look into our crystal ball to describe the issues that multinational firms will face. In our last chapter, we condense the collected tips of this book into one ready reference.

I
LEADING YOURSELF

1

THE RISE AND RISE OF ASIA PACIFIC

A little over a quarter century ago, entrepreneurs in South Asia began to quietly change the world.

Turn the clock back to 1981. The top story of the year was the attempted assassination of Ronald Reagan, who began his first term as US President. After a period of détente, the cold war against the "Evil Empire" of the Soviet Union was heating up again, East and West Germany were still divided and the Berlin Wall still stood, and Soviet occupation put an obscure country called Afghanistan onto the front pages of Western newspapers.

No newspaper recorded the day when N.R. Narayana Murthy and six others pooled together US$250 and created a company in Bangalore, India, that would help forever change the way business is done.

Growing up in the socialist dynamic of India, Murthy graduated from the Indian Institute of Technology in the 1960s with views "that all rich people were out to exploit the poor in all circumstances," he recalled in an interview with the *Wall Street Journal*. After a stint working in Europe, he came back to India believing that poverty "had to be solved by creating more jobs, creating more wealth. The only way to do that is entrepreneurship."

Inspired by a lecture from a visiting Princeton University professor, he focused his future on writing software. But it was hardscrabble from the start, he told the *Wall Street Journal Asia* (November 5, 2004)—he traveled by bicycle to see his first client. Trying to import a computer required 25 trips to New Delhi to obtain government permits in the closed Indian economy of the 1980s. But his diligence paid off in ways unimaginable at the time. The company Murthy helped create, Infosys Technologies Ltd., practically invented business process outsourcing, creating specialized software programs to streamline business operations for Fortune 500 companies around the world.

Along the way, those seven founders created a company that employs nearly 100,000 people, has US$4 billion in revenues, and helped put the city of Bangalore into the consciousness of business leaders around the world. "I am very happy we have created a [role] model which has enthused literally millions of entrepreneurs, to show them it's possible to run a business legally and ethically... in India," Murthy added.

Just as the humble beginning of Infosys in Bangalore passed unnoticed by the world press, a scan of major newspapers in 1981 finds scant mention of the Chinese city of Shenzhen. "China Seeks to Lure Investors to Shekou Industrial Site" says a tiny notice buried in the pages of the *Wall Street Journal*, referring to an industrial park in Shenzhen that China "hopes to be a magnet for foreign investment." A small fishing village where the Pearl River pours into the South China Sea, Shenzhen was made the first special economic zone by Deng Xiaoping, starting the Middle Kingdom down the road away from Maoist-style planned economy and toward free market practices.

The magnetic pull of Shenzhen was first limited to investors from neighboring Hong Kong and laborers from the rural Chinese countryside. But soon, the world was attracted to Shenzhen. One out of every eight mobile phones in the world was produced in Shenzhen, and export increased 150 percent—with a total of nearly 26 million phones shipped—in the first half of 2007, according to a report by Shenzhen Customs reported in the *SinoCast China Business Daily* (July 19, 2006). The same article indicated that the Shenzhen Watch and Clock Association reported that half of the timepieces made in the world in the past four years were manufactured in Shenzhen, along with half of the world's eyeglasses.

The cities of Shenzhen in China and Bangalore in India represent the new poles of the growing power of Asia to the business world. The brains of Bangalore and the manufacturing brawn of Shenzhen are the twin axes of the burgeoning development happening in economies around the region. They are the leading edge of the second wave of Asia's impact on the global business world. The first wave was Japan's world-changing manufacturing practices, which helped the country rise after World War II to become the world's second-largest economy with its titanic automotive and electronic consumer goods industries. This second wave is a tsunami—the titanic forces of China and India, the world's most populous nations, are causing sweeping changes around the globe.

Technology and globalization are rewriting the rules for 21st-century business. Both have opened rich new veins of products to sell and places to sell them. The playing field has been leveled across borders. Technology has changed the way business is done and what customers expect from it—the demand for better services and products at lower prices has never been greater, and will only grow. This has created a razor's edge of opportunity and pitfall for modern managers. Companies can collapse or grow at astonishing speeds.

The chain of value created by offshore technology and service providers is immense and significantly (or "greatly") responsive to opportunities. Offshoring was once just call centers and computer programming, now it is radiologists, newspaper editing and stock trading. The recent problems of investment banks on Wall Street have been a boon for financial data providers in India. In China, particularly in the areas near Hong Kong whose economies first opened, business is evolving away from an original equipment manufacturing (OEM) base to high-value goods and services. Two Shenzhen companies born in the boom—ZTE Corporation and Huawei—are global technology makers in their own right. These companies and their leaders are hungry, smart and quick to react to the global market—a dangerous combination for their competitors in the West.

Yet a crisis is emerging in the Asia Pacific region.

Asia Pacific Companies Go Global

As the economies of India, China, and the rest of the region blossom, multinational companies scramble for executive talent to meet the breakneck pace of change. Yet the floor is dropping beneath them: the post-World War II Baby Boomer generation is retiring faster than the executive pool can be refilled.

Shortages caused by the twin forces of demographics and economic expansion may not slow the pace of change. But they will force an increasing demand for transcultural and transgenerational diversity among executive teams.

What is a novelty today will be a way of life tomorrow.

In a post-expatriate era, the biggest demand is for qualified and experienced local executives. Established multinational firms are now competing with rising Asian companies to find in-country executives who are able to straddle different ethnic and corporate cultures. These executives also need to know how to lead a workforce that spans five generations of people with widely diverging priorities and values.

The macroeconomic picture is frightening. Within 10 years, the oil needs of China and India alone will take the entire output of the Organization of Petroleum Exporting Countries (OPEC). China is estimated to need at least 75,000 business leaders in the next 10 years, but the present supply is fewer than 5,000. Multinational executives say that barely 10 percent of local managers are qualified to work in their organizations.

Being a CEO these days is a risky business. Recent surveys show that the number of CEOs terminated due to poor performance is up 70 percent from 10 years ago. Very few 55-plus-year-old chief executives have global experience, though the 45-plus age group represents an increasing number of executives with the experience and education to take a more globally integrated view of their business. Former BHP Billiton CEO Chip Goodyear says there is a "huge shortage" of executive talent available for global deployment—"and it's not going to get any easier any time soon."

Heidrick & Struggles conducted a series of interviews with chief executives and business experts across the region to find out the challenges companies face as they expand business in a globalized world.

The multinational companies we spoke with vary widely by size and industry. BHP Billiton, the world's largest mining firm (headquartered in Melbourne and dual-listed on the London Stock Exchange), is a well-known globalist. But smaller companies such as the hearing implant maker Cochlear and explosives supplier Orica are achieving global dominance in niche markets. New Zealand's Fonterra and Sealord are expanding rapidly in the dairy and seafood sectors.

Out of Hong Kong, food and beverage producer Vitasoy has expanded into the United States, China, Europe, Australia, New Zealand, and South America, and Lark International is active in clothing, dairy, property, multimedia, food, and beverage and investments in North America and Asia.

At the board level, globalizing companies are still reluctant to appoint foreign nationals who understand the markets they are seeking to win. For example, while only 30 percent of a Japanese motor company's revenues may come from domestic markets, 13 of the 14 board members will be Japanese. Similar disparities are to be found in most globalizing companies.

Experts say that such pre-globalization thinking does not allow new ideas and values to percolate at the board level and down through the top management level.

Most of the CEOs we talked with were optimistic about the future, but emphasized that huge cultural challenges would face the incoming executive teams. As one told us: "The thinking of executives will have to change at a greater pace than currently being exhibited. The new dogs will have to learn many more tricks than the old dogs and be good at teaching these tricks as well."

Talent Exported

Why is the world's most populous and prosperous region suffering from a shortage of skilled people? The major factors involve changing global demographics at a time of Asia Pacific economic expansion.

Experienced and qualified executives from Western countries are becoming scarce as the Baby Boomers retire. The European Union fears—as do most developed economies—that its replacement workforce will not meet the needs of its aging population. *The Economist* (July 26, 2007) reports that by 2030, Japan will have only two working-age people for each retired one. Europe is predicting a workforce deficit of up to 100 million, while the United States is forecasting a deficit of between 25 million and 48 million.

Meanwhile, youthful populations are expanding in the Middle East. More than 50 percent of Saudi Arabia's 13 million population is under the age of 18, while over 65 percent of Iran's well-educated youth are unemployed.

Across Asia Pacific, the pool of top talent has simply been fished out. Much of the top tier of local talent around the region has gone overseas and stayed there. CEOs interviewed say the era of expatriate or "parachutist" executives dropped into offshore markets is fast coming to a close, intensifying the demand for local executives.

In India, the competition for executives has pushed compensation packages toward parity with international peers. Mumbai-based India Infoline invested more than US$10 million in sign-on bonuses to get four executives from France's Credit Lyonnais to help set up its investment banking division.[1]

Turnover of top executives can also be high, particularly in the information technology and consulting market. Companies are buying up competitors to acquire skill sets and expand market share.

The leadership challenges go beyond functional needs. According to Professor Christopher Bartlett of Harvard University's Global Leadership Faculty, those companies best at "accessing the scarce resources of intellectual and human capital" will gain sustainable competitive advantage in a "flat earth" business era.[2]

Bartlett has seen it all. A former marketing executive with Alcoa in Australia, a management consultant at McKinsey and Company in London, and a general manager at Baxter Laboratories' subsidiary company in France, Bartlett believes that the most critical attribute in a global executive is open-mindedness, or what he calls "the ability to see that differences in other cultures are strengths, not obstacles."

Executives who are driving global strategies from head offices must also be capable of developing strong leadership teams overseas, CEOs interviewed said. These teams must be infused with the corporate culture of the foreign arrival—and conversely, the globalizing company needs to understand the culture of its new market.

The executives of today's Asia Pacific region must also celebrate cultural differences, and have a keen eye to find and nurture emerging talent. Succession planning must be a top priority.

Cultural Flexibility and Corporate Tights

Infosys co-founder and co-chairman Nandan Nilekani tells us that he frequently brings large groups of Western-trained executives to India in order to imbue them with the corporate culture before sending them back into offshore markets. Infosys also fast-tracks potential executives, giving them experience in different overseas divisions.

Corporate cultural values are what Kirby Adams, former CEO of steelmaker BlueScope, calls "the cultural tights"—or values that are nonnegotiable. "It doesn't matter where we are, one of our tights is a certain safety culture and a certain environmental culture," he says. "Once you understand your tights, you can customize your strategy for local markets and make sure your executives understand them."

The Asia Pacific region's expansion has been a key driver of global prosperity, and it is still picking up steam. According to the International Monetary Fund, the region will account for 45 percent of world gross domestic product (GDP) by 2015, compared with 20 percent for the United States and 17 percent for Western Europe. Some bold moves have been taken in the quest for new markets. Lenovo, which had not sold a single computer outside its home market of China until

2006, now has customers in 66 countries and one of the world's best distribution systems after acquiring IBM's personal computer division and moving its headquarters to Raleigh, North Carolina.[3]

Former Lenovo chief financial officer Mary Ma, who was involved in the negotiations with IBM, says of American William Amelio's appointment as CEO of Lenovo: "We didn't send a successful guy from China to head it up. We wanted to have the best people in the industry who understood the local market."

Amelio, who has since moved on, formerly served served as president of Dell in Japan and the Asia Pacific region.

Ma says that one of the biggest difficulties for Western executives working with their Chinese team is cultural difference rather than language difference. "For example, differences in communications styles are to be expected. An oversimplification is that the Western style is characterized by talking, understanding, and listening. The Asian style starts with listening, understanding, and then talking. Therefore, we strongly encouraged our staff in China to be more outspoken at meetings, so as to share their views and opinions. On the other hand, we encouraged our foreign staff to listen to their China counterparts' views at meetings."

The Modern Global Executive

Globalization expert Professor George Foster of Stanford University told us that executives in companies that operate in two or three different continents need to possess a range of abilities and aptitudes that are often difficult to find in the talent pool.[4]

Foster, who directs the Executive Program for Growing Companies at Stanford's Graduate School of Business, says that global executives need to

- Enjoy dealing with different cultures—not just tolerate them.
- Have a global outlook.
- Enjoy ambiguity and management paradoxes—"change requires stability" and the like.
- Have the ability to cope with the tensions that accompany a 24/7, globe-hopping job.

"If you're operating in the United States, Australia, or a time zone in Europe, then the clock never stops," Foster says. "You need to develop a way of handling the job 24 hours a day. That's not an easy thing for some executives who are used to being in total control all the time."

Foster also says that global executives need to delegate more "and to have some pretty good rules in terms of what problems have to be surfaced right to the top and what problems should really be handled at the continental level or the country level."

Many companies expanding offshore are aware of the talent shortage and are grooming leaders within their organizations. Leadership assessment and coaching is seen as increasingly important. But there is no substitute for experience, and the pool of experienced executives is vanishing. Executives we interviewed were concerned about the looming shortage of skilled leaders, and the availability of future executives and senior managers.

The Use of Expatriates

The "expat era" is changing rapidly. Globalizing companies "need to dismiss the idea that the best inventions are at home and we're going to parachute our own people with our own cultures and beliefs," BHP Billiton's Goodyear says.

Expatriates receiving salary supplements and additional benefits such as home leave, school tuition, and a housing subsidy can cost a company at least double what a local executive would cost. Expat assignments are declining not only because they cost so much but also because expatriates are not good mentors of local talent; they tend to leave little in the way of legacy.

Fonterra CEO Andrew Ferrier says the company's original business model was "to drop expats in all over the world." There are still a reasonable number of New Zealanders in the dairy company's global offices, "but certainly, we have recognized that in the majority of the countries we're in, that's not a sustainable model," he says.

Lark International's chairman and CEO David Tso says that many expatriates lack commitment. "They are highly paid but not committed to the business or to the region. During my time with various companies, I have had to fire several executives—including five managers, three directors, and one chairman."

Chief executives emphasize that cross-border cultural understanding on the part of leaders in their offshore markets is a major factor dictating the pace of expansion. With the right leaders in place, they can gain competitive advantage. With the wrong ones, companies can lose valuable time while rivals defend their turf and capture market share.

During our CEO talks, five main themes emerged:

- Establish a beachhead. As companies establish their initial offshore presence in the host nation, they ship executives from the home country to learn the vagaries of the new market.
- Face the challenge of cultural differences. Differences in national cultures are evaluated and efforts are made to address them.
- Find local talent for local operations. Executives are brought on board from the host country as the company expands beyond the exploratory phase. Then the trick is to retain the smartest executives who learn quickly from the newcomer and thus increase their market value.
- Export the corporate culture. As the corporate culture is regarded as just as important to the company's long-term success as the culture in which the operation is now immersed, efforts are made to instill the values into the new host nation executives.
- Develop global leaders. Executives from both home and target countries must be given "global" experience to enhance the organization's flexibility and competitiveness.

Establishing the Beachhead

Both Nilekani of Infosys and former BlueScope boss Adams say the key role for executives in global companies is to build a scalable business model that will work in multiple countries and then convey that model to the teams in the host nations. "Of course the executives must focus on building a brand, because as they go international, they need to ensure the company has brand recall and brand awareness in the minds of customers as well as potential employees in the local market," Nilekani says.

The first phase in offshore expansion is "very sales- and marketing-oriented," Adams says, and typically starts with a mix of expatriates and local executives from the building materials industry who are aware of BlueScope Steel products. This then establishes a platform for further growth.

When working through a global strategy to be implemented in a different culture, the main quality needed by the executive is patience, Adams says. "It's a real virtue—not one of mine normally! And it is a virtue you need in the Asian markets, which are more challenging than the Australian market. You need to protect your technology and know when to pull out, if necessary."

Former Lenovo executive Ma says the company sends Chinese people into markets in the United States, France and Singapore to help build the transactional model used successfully in China and to marry it with the relationship model that helped build IBM's market share. "But the Chinese do not act as leaders in those countries—we have locals at the top, who work with the team from China. And of course the Chinese learn a lot about how to do business in foreign countries. There are benefits for both groups."

Vitasoy CEO Ambrose Chan says that personal trust is crucial in the initial phase. When his soy milk company moved from its Hong Kong base into mainland China and Europe, it took many years and many millions of dollars to establish a beachhead. "I have to say the number one importance for international expansion is people," he says. "You have to get the right people at the top. The next thing is to find suitable partners locally to set up strategic alliances. They need to understand your brand values and have a commitment for the future."

Facing the Challenge of Cultural Differences

The major cultural difference between Western and Chinese companies relates to authority.

"If there's a debate in a Western company, the leader will often leave it to the managers to work it through," Ma says. "But in China, the issue will be presented to the CEO who will make a final decision. If you come along and present the Chinese managers with an ambiguity, they will feel very frustrated that the leader will not make a decision."

BHP Billiton's CEO Goodyear says that resources companies are scouring the world for talent. "But if you think you can just hire someone and assume that they know your culture, your organization, their job responsibilities, and how to work in a different culture or different environment, you're kidding yourself."

He says the managerial and technical talent needed to run global businesses "will take many, many years to develop."

Orica—a company that began as a 19th-century explosives supplier to Australian goldfields—is now diversified into mining, consumer products, and chemical industries operating in 50 nations. The company built its far-ranging empire by learning to build a mix of nationalities and skills in offshore leadership teams.

CEO Graeme Liebelt says executives need to be sensitive to cultural differences.

"It's about mind-set. A CEO or any international manager needs to understand that different cultures operate in different ways—that one culture is not 'better or worse' than any other culture," he says. "The secret of success actually is to build on the strengths of those cultures and use them to reinforce the business strategy that you're seeking to undertake."

Liebelt gives the example of Australian executives working in South America. "The Latin Americans quite like authority, but they are much stronger about relationships and so their culture is more energetic and excitable. In some ways, you can spark that off to use it to reinforce creativity. But if you seek to impose on them in an unthinking way—which is the Australian way of operating—Latin Americans do not react well to that."

He says that while Australians have a reputation as straightforward, cut-to-the-chase people, this approach does not work well in all cultures.

"We're egalitarian, consultative, and open to the point where people challenge authority. We will have the discussion but then we're decisive. In Latin America, people love to be consulted and once you make a decision, they will follow that decision to the best of their ability. In Scandinavia, there is a lot more work that needs to be done to get everybody on the same page. There is a much more democratic process of decision making. Australians consult, but they're not democratic in the process of making a decision. In Germany, they are very uncomfortable with how open and challenging of authority we are. The decision making is not very open and democratic. So the Scandinavians clash with the Germans for that reason."

BlueScope's Adams says that what works in one country may not work in another—each country and market is different, sometimes radically so. Or as he puts it: "Asia is not 'Asia.'"

Finding Local Talent for Local Operations

Infosys initially used Indian nationals in its international markets, Nilekani recalls.

"But over time, we have tried to make our company more multicultural and today, in many of the markets, it's a combination of Indian nationals and local employees. In many of the countries in which we operate, the head of the operation is a local person. In Australia, we have a subsidiary, Infosys Australia, which came about through the merger with a local company—so it's very much an Australian company with a mix of local Australian employees and Indian nationals." He says the aim is to have a local presence, local people, and local culture, and to combine the best of Infosys culture with the local culture and mores of the host country.

Chan of Vitasoy adds that local executives in local markets are important for an understanding of local laws and the consumer behavior of the target market.

Different parts of the business call for different approaches, according to Fonterra's Ferrier. "In our pure trading business—ingredients trading—sometimes a Kiwi at the top works well. If you're in our consumer product business and it's about understanding consumer drives, consumer interests, and so on in various different geographies, you need a huge number of locals."

Ferrier says that while the China business is headed up by a New Zealander, immediately under him is a Hong Kong Chinese senior manager who speaks Cantonese and Mandarin, with several Mandarin-speaking Chinese in senior management roles. Orica's Liebelt says that "all things being equal, we try to get locals," and that in working out the competencies needed for executives, international experience is at the top of the list.

Orica has a Scandinavian at the head of its European business, an American running North America, and an Australian running Australia and Asia.

Dr. Chris Roberts, CEO of the hearing device company Cochlear, says locals work best—if you can get them. "You want a Frenchman to run France and you want a German to run Germany, you want a Swede to run Sweden and ideally an American to run America. But that's not to say you can't move people around a bit."

He says the single biggest problem for executives in an international business "always was and always will be" communication.

"My approach is to have strong regional presidents in Asia Pacific, Europe, and the United States, but to make sure that they are really good at communication. If you have good communication at the top, you can push and force it down through the organization. But if you don't have good communication at the top, you won't get good communication through the organization very easily. Having said that, I've also seen that communication can be a problem between the 39th and 40th floor in a building."

BlueScope's Adams says its target country executives need to become part of the local business community, sometimes buying steel for its products from local companies rather than sourcing it from

Australia. The executives need to build ties with universities, local architects and planning bodies.

"Good relationships with government officials can also be important," Adams says. In some countries, BlueScope has had to ask regulators to change building codes just to allow steel to be used in applications such as roofing.

BlueScope also has a policy of more than 90 percent local staff in its target country. Adams says the challenge for his company as well as many others is to retain the local executives once they are up to speed. "In China, the competition for talent is fairly intense and people who have, say, five years' experience with an Australian blue-chip like BlueScope can pretty easily lever that into a role with a multinational. There's a big demand now for Chinese who have experience in Western corporate governance."

Exporting the Corporate Culture

Lenovo's Ma says that turning around the underperforming personal computer business bought from IBM has been possible only through executives in the overseas markets being able to implement Lenovo's successful sales strategy.

"Lenovo adopts a dual business model approach, which was developed and refined in China. Based on different customer needs and preferences in products, service, and buying channels, Lenovo first segmented customers into two types—relationship and transaction—and built complementary business models accordingly," Ma says.

"The transaction business model is the hallmark of Lenovo's success in China. It is a product-driven model that best serves customers who want to get the latest PC technology and be able to touch the product," she says. "This 'push' model satisfies a group of customers' key and common requirements, usually small and medium-sized businesses and consumers. Product marketing is the key to driving sales in the transaction model."

"On the other hand, the relationship model is a customer-driven one based on customer uniqueness, satisfying the individual customer's specific requirements," she adds. "It is a 'pull' model that leverages Lenovo's direct relationship with large enterprise customers by delivering stable technology and tailored configuration products."

While employing host-country executives, Lenovo sends Chinese executives to help establish the business model, as well as to learn how to do business in different cultures.

Infosys's Nilekani agrees that exporting the successful corporate culture is critical. "We want somebody who can be a strong leader in the host countries, who can be the face of the company, who can be the ambassador and custodian of our values, who can really put the point of view of our business proposition across to customers. At the same time, we want somebody who understands the global Indian Infosys ethos, how it works, so that they bridge the two," he says. "If you're managing a company which has a global footprint, diverse nationalities, diverse clients, diverse all over the place, the values of the company are really the bedrock—the glue which holds the firm together."

Cochlear's Roberts says the company bought a Swedish manufacturing business and serves it through a visiting Australian executive, whose primary role is to instill the corporate culture into the local operation. "We wanted to keep it Swedish, but we wanted to make sure that they understood our culture."

Developing Global Leaders

Tso of Lark International says the key to developing leaders in China is to shake up their natural instinct not to challenge authority. "Because I was born and raised in Taiwan and moved to Rochester in New York, I bring those kinds of Western concepts to our young tigers," he says. "You walk with them, eat with them and chat with them in daily business so they can grow very fast. They learn your style and your thinking very quickly. You need to let them make mistakes and correct them afterwards."

Referring to a previous stint with Kodak in China, Tso says that leadership talent is not lacking in Beijing or Shanghai, but due to the historic and cultural gap, the potential executives tend to be followers. "We have to encourage them to think and make decisions and take the initiative."

Ma says there are many "smart, excellent" Chinese executives—"and the thing that everyone needs to improve is communication, if they want to operate in a global market." Orica's Liebelt adds that for someone to reach the top in his company, they need to gain international experience—"not just so that they can learn the many different ways of operating in different cultures, but because it opens their minds to the differences they will encounter as they work with different cultures."

The development of leaders starts with the selection process, Liebelt says. "Business is fundamentally a creative process—you can't succeed without creating things that your customers want," he says. "So the trick for an international business like ours is to find and develop leaders who can draw on the strengths of the different cultures. We want executives who can communicate effectively in different places, to transfer what we know and love of America, for example, to Europe, and vice versa."

According to BHP Billiton's Goodyear there is no single solution to the problem. "You need a sprinkling of all types of cultures and skills and talents—so usually, even in a new place, one size doesn't fit all," he says. "Our goal is to identify good people early on, bring them out of the country where they grew up and went to school, and then get them to know the world and our company by working internationally. When we bring them back to their home country later on, they are indoctrinated with our culture and have new horizons—a global mind-set."

For smaller multinationals such as Cochlear, the starting point is to engage executives who are self-starters. "While the need is to be good strategic thinkers, they also need to be able to execute," says CEO Roberts. "They need to have integrity, because if you have people out in the back of nowhere, you have to be able to trust them."

What's the Answer?

In the short term, the solution to the current and future shortage of top executive talent will be increasing waves of executive migration across the countries of Asia Pacific. As the need for human capital expands, governments will respond to the demands of business for more liberal policies to encourage the movement of talent.

Companies will seek the best people from both developing nations and mature Asian economies. This will spark a compensation war as Asia Pacific countries try to both keep their locals and poach talent from Western countries, and Western countries respond in kind. Companies will need to listen closely to the needs of their leadership talent—not just their compensation needs, but also helping them develop a fulfilling career and lifestyle.

The best people are those who demonstrate flexibility, emotional intelligence, and innovation. These leaders and potential leaders will be looking to their employers to display similar flexibility toward them in their career and life plans.

Chief executives in Asia Pacific are already experiencing leadership pressures and are taking steps to lead robust talent management strategies such as these:

- Exposing executives to deeper levels of strategy making and business planning to create development opportunities for them.
- Recognizing that people's long-term career and life aspirations are inextricably linked and moving to assist where possible.
- Rewarding top talent in more creative ways. For example, some banks are offering executives the choice of 75 percent of full pay for a yearlong leave after four years on the job to pursue other interests (write a book, start a business).
- Developing the management team to appreciate and respond to the emerging demands of leadership across the five generations that will be simultaneously employed by organizations to meet their needs over the next 10 years.

Global leaders in today's flat world need to be humble. They need to eschew ethnocentricity and see cultural differences as building blocks of innovation and ideas from which their business can benefit.

Asian leaders need to ask themselves what they can learn from Australian or European sustainability and environmental trends, and Western leaders need to approach Asian consumers as eager trendsetters who can teach them more about their own products than they can learn in their more mature home markets.

The scarcest resource is inside the minds of the leaders of tomorrow—not just their knowledge and network of superb business relationships, but the objectivity and flexibility of character that will enable them to seize opportunities in the uncertain future.

Endnotes

1 "Leadership Challenges Emerge as Asia Pacific Companies Go Global," a white paper published by Heidrick & Struggles, March 2008.
2 Ibid.
3 Ibid.
4 Ibid.

2

THE EVOLVING C-SUITE

A chairman's nightmare goes something like this: You're nine to 12 months away from the chief executive's retirement date. You have identified an outstanding internal candidate, someone who seems better each time you look. But at the last minute, this executive departs. You then move to your fallback candidate.

Within a few months, you know you have made a mistake. An acquisition goes wrong, an unforeseen issue erupts in an unwatched part of the business, and suddenly you're looking at tens of millions of dollars in unplanned contingencies (losses). The company's reputation has suffered and the competition is taking advantage of the turmoil. Your turkey gets an undeserved golden parachute and you have to start the process of succession planning all over again. Meantime, other promising candidates have left for more stable environments.

It's an expensive learning curve.

CEO Succession

While the term *succession planning* has been bandied about for many years, a truly rigorous and objective approach has been neglected in favor of what we might loosely call "replacement planning," where the favored son or daughter has been anointed or "given the nod." Until recently, most CEOs were internal rather than external appointments. Often, the outgoing CEO chooses a mirror image to be the next in line. This type of well-intentioned paternalism has had its day—the talents that grew the business in the past are unlikely to carry it into the future.

Succession is not just a task—the replacement of an executive—but a process whose immediate focus is risk management and whose longer-term aim is strategic competitive advantage. CEOs must move away from building relationships primarily with doers, that is, with people who can help them execute. Instead, they must forge new alliances with stakeholders including institutional investors, analysts, governments, media, unions, and regulatory authorities. They need to be comfortable with ambiguity and able to balance beliefs and views opposed to their own. They need to listen and consult, and then to execute with boldness and vision, in the full glare of investor and media scrutiny.

Graham Kraehe, chairman of Brambles and BlueScope Steel, says that after a systematic succession process, both companies settled on experienced internal executives who had a vision for the company—but with a grounded, realistic approach. "They saw the current strengths and weaknesses of the businesses and were able to articulate how they would address those issues and opportunities," Kraehe says. "They showed a greater willingness to challenge the status quo.... They recognized that things could be done better and they had a clear view on how to go about enhancing performance going forward."

External Versus Internal

In the past, the rule of thumb for a chairman when looking at the "external" versus "internal" argument has been a simple if-then equation:

- If the company is performing well and you intend to stay on a path consistent with the experience of the existing chief executive, then an internal appointment is often the most appropriate.
- If things are going badly and cultural change or a new brand positioning is called for, then an external appointment, with a different set of biases to bring to bear on the problem, is often the most appropriate.

But the systematic analysis of available talent by outside consultants is unearthing a depth of potential leaders not previously brought to the notice of boards. Chairman Michael Chaney of National Australia Bank says that proper planning and transparency of the process are also vital to avoid politicking and perceptions of favoritism. Chaney, the former Wesfarmers CEO, worked with external professionals and his board there to orchestrate a successful transition to Richard Goyder.

Chairman Bob Savage of David Jones says the succession planning process is an inside-out game. "You need to look both outside and within the organization. You should always consider the best internal candidate and you should benchmark them against what's available on the outside."

The Plan

A successful succession plan is a four-step process, driven by the board and supported by external professionals:

1. Inclusive analysis and planning, bringing together all key stakeholders from board members to investors.
2. Internal and external candidate identification and preparation, with all candidates compared on the same basis.
3. Decision, with transparency and full communication with stakeholders, shareholders, and board. Like the photo finish in a tight horse race, this transparency can reveal in close-up what might not be obvious from a distance.
4. Transition to the CEO suite, with advisory coaching and sustained "on-boarding" to ensure the executive is comfortable with any new aspects of the game.

Consolation Prizes

How do chairmen handle bruised egos when qualified executives miss out on the top job?

Chaney says, "While you might hope that the people who are going to miss out secretly harbor the desire not to get the job because they realize their skills lie elsewhere, the fact is they are likely to be devastated." Kraehe adds that much can be done to minimize the fallout, such as shorter-term incentives (12 months maximum) and opportunities for learning. "The worst scenario is to have an appointment announced, and within days or weeks, you have defections. The message to the unsuccessful executive should be: 'You fell short in a couple of areas and we want to work with you to give you some business experience or development to build up those areas. While we hope you will stay with us long term, if you elect to go somewhere else, you are going to be better prepared for it.'"

If the runners-up can be retained for 12 months, the new chief's team will be solidly in place and any defections will be less damaging.

Properly done succession processes ensure that new chief executives thrive and prosper at what is potentially the most challenging time of anyone's life. As they experience the shock of the cliché "lonely at the top" syndrome and are tested in all sorts of new ways, CEOs will enter their new role in the knowledge that whatever the challenges may be, they have the skills and techniques to deal with them. At the same time, board members collectively uncross their fingers, confident that a systematic and rigorous process has been followed and the new chief has the best possible support in place to carry the business forward.

A Heartbeat from the Top: Chief Operating Officer

While there is no generally accepted definition of the role of the chief operating officer (COO), Rupert Murdoch expressed a popular view when he responded to analysts' questions about his succession plans: "In the unlikely event that I should prove to be mortal, Peter Chernin will take over the running of News Corporation."

Chernin, the New York-born book editor who transformed the Fox Network and became COO while he was at News Corporation, is a good example of the second-in-command model, complementing Murdoch's business acumen with an ability to run a team. While the role of COO is not always that of "deputy CEO," there are usually few executives better qualified to take the reins in the event of the death or sudden departure of the CEO.

The challenge in discussing the COO's role is that its scope varies widely. In *Riding Shotgun: The Role of the COO* (Stanford Business Books), former Microsoft COO Bob Herbold says the role has no single descriptor. "There are a number of ways to assemble responsibilities in a way that creates a job that can easily carry that title," he says in the book, which was written by Heidrick & Struggles partner Stephen Miles with Georgia Institute of Technology professor Nathan Bennett. "At Microsoft, my job was to handle the business issues... while Steve Ballmer [the CEO] ran sales and I worked for Bill [Gates, the founder and chairman] to handle all the business issues so as to keep them out of Bill's hair." That left Gates free to run the product group.

Broadly speaking, it is possible to describe the role of the COO as a *head-down* position, focused on the operational details and day-to-day execution necessary for success, while the CEO is a *head-up* role looking outward with a strategic view to make sure the business does not miss changes in the industry and technology. The CEO must also spend considerable time engaging shareholders and media to help create the corporate brand and reputation.

While Miles and Bennett in *Riding Shotgun* say there could be as many as six different types of COO, three major styles can easily be identified:

- *Mentor:* Dell Computer founder Michael Dell hired Mort Topfer to help accelerate his own development as leader at a time when the growth of his company was threatening to get ahead of his managerial experience. Similarly, Heidrick & Struggles recruited Eric Schmidt to support Google founders Larry Page and Sergey Brin as the incredibly successful Internet search engine went from start-up to operational, then into an expansion phase.
- *Change agent:* Ray Lane was hired by Oracle founder Larry Ellison to help turn around the company's troubled sales and marketing organizations. Before falling out with Ellison, Lane drove sales from US$1 billion to US$10 billion, tripling net profits. The late Kerry Packer hired "Chainsaw" Al Dunlap to transform a moribund Publishing and Broadcasting Limited culture and dispose of noncore assets.
- *Partner:* Often called "two in a box," this type of COO role requires an executive willing to forsake an ambition for the top job. It works well in family companies, such as leading Australian defense and technology contractor Tenix.

While the performance metrics for the COO role vary, the qualities remain constant. Trust and humility are the key characteristics. When there is trust, and both CEO and COO know their place, the result is a strong profit-driving team. Where there is competition and lack of trust, you will eventually have disruption and instability, as at Oracle. Liebelt says that people are the major focus of a CEO as opposed to a COO. "The time split would be around a quarter on senior people issues, a quarter on media and shareholders, and the balance on strategic issues with the board and a bit of operational stuff on top of that."

It Takes Two: Chief Financial Officer

When things go wrong at the top of major corporations, it isn't long before the blowtorch turns on the chief executive officer, and then almost as rapidly on to the chief financial officer (CFO).

Often, the CFO hasn't been in step with the vision of the CEO, or has glanced away from the main game to help pursue "big picture" strategies. But the best story in financial services in Australia is to be found in the successful synergy of the top CEOs and their CFOs. When that relationship works well, profits and performance follow.

There was a time, not too long ago, when more often than not the CFO was the bearer of bad news, characterized by such dismal phrases as "we're not going to make budget" or "we need to cut costs." Today's CFO, however, is more of a strategic enabler at the top of the corporation. The role today reflects a wider picture, with good CFOs having a deep understanding of how to achieve the chief executive's vision.

When former Insurance Australia Group (IAG) CEO Michael Hawker was asked, "What makes an admirable CEO?" he pointed to his then CFO, George Venardos. The growth that Hawker set out to achieve when he took the helm at the insurer after a distinguished career at Westpac was orchestrated largely through the support of his CFO. To give just one example, within two years of its takeover of SGIO, IAG had increased premium revenue from the acquired company by a third, achieved cost reductions of US$10 million a year, and increased the enterprise value of the combined businesses by more than 30 percent.

IAG's Hawker says the role of the CFO has changed considerably since the days of the simple number-cruncher. "The CFO's core responsibility is to understand and analyze the raw figures better than anyone else in the organization," he says. "This confidence in technical capability builds trust between the two executives, which is essential in any working relationship." But Hawker says that providing transparent and accurate data is not enough: "There has to be an ability to convert the data into action.... For example, IAG's strategic goals of enhancing shareholder return, providing return on equity, and maintaining our insurer financial strength ratings could not even have been planned without George Venardos playing this role."

Hawker says that top CFOs should be well-rounded and able to manage the people within the finance function of an organization. "Managing a large team is an extremely difficult task, which is why personal skills are so vital."

UBS banking research head Jeff Emmanuel agrees that the most successful executives of financial services companies have a symbiotic relationship where the CFO provides the information that the CEO needs for optimal execution. "Things go wrong at the top when the CFO is not able to translate his financial acumen into something that assists with improved running of the company," says Emmanuel.

"Even if he's a good accountant, he must also be able to extrapolate that into information to help support better decisions."

Emmanuel says a CFO's deep understanding of risk management is pivotal for corporate success in the financial sector. He lists these characteristics of symbiotic CEOs and CFOs:

CEO
- Strategic vision
- Ability to unfold that vision into achievable tasks
- Ability to motivate and encourage the senior management team

CFO
- Financial understanding of the company's activities
- Ability to clearly communicate the business outcomes
- Ability to explain the operations of the business and its progress
- Awareness and appreciation of key drivers and risks

What makes CFOs good? "They don't sleep much," says JP Morgan's chief banking analyst, Brian Johnson. "They are on top of all the issues affecting their industry. They have an incredible knowledge of the wider environment, and have a high work ethic. They are able to develop and implement a strategy and then communicate it clearly."

Johnson says the best CFOs are not afraid to listen to alternative views. They are not interested in a culture of self-denial, but are interested in self-criticism and improvement. "But the key to driving a company forward into transformational change is usually that the two key people at the top of the company are in lockstep, with total unity of vision and purpose."

The Rise of Strategic HR: Chief Human Resources Officer

The field of human resources has changed dramatically. Formerly focused on process and administration, the job of the chief human resources officer (CHRO) is now focused on behavioral science and ways to get organizations and individuals to behave in different and more effective ways. US and European companies are coming to grips with the new role of HR, but Asian companies are lagging far behind in appreciating how HR has changed and how strategic CHROs have become.

New Directions

In a sense, HR is splitting in two. One piece is the administrative, transactional work, which is becoming more automated: payroll, compensation and benefits, training and development, and similar activities are moving to shared service centers or specialized internal resources. That leaves the other piece, the strategic, organizational development function, that is key to helping a company figure out how to get from A to B with respect to talent. This aspect of HR is becoming metrics-driven, with business schools and other training establishments trying to equip CHROs and measure their contributions against corporate needs.

Great transformational and strategic roles are ahead. Unfortunately, Asia has an alarming shortage of truly able HR people to fill the strategic role of CHRO. Most of Asia's HR people are mired in the old ways of thinking about HR's role. They have not been trained and conditioned to work with and to influence top-tier management. Likewise, management does not see HR as a business partner. This has a lot to do with the traditional hands-on approach to people issues that characterizes Asian management teams, unlike their counterparts in the United States or Europe. Unfortunately it is an issue of chicken and egg: until corporate leaders see the impact a truly great HR executive can have, they are dubious about thinking of HR in anything but traditional terms.

The most effective CHRO understands a company's business strategy and puts good systems and people in place to ensure that their organization is, from a talent perspective, staffed to cope with today's fierce business environment. They concentrate on people—building bench strength, coaching, and ensuring success. They hold line managers accountable for their performance in conserving and developing the people who report to them. Many of the traditional functions of HR management (compensation and benefits, training, and so on) are given to somebody with another title or outsourced, freeing HR to focus on the really important business of talent management.

The War for Talent

Without doubt, a real battle to attract, develop, retain, and motivate talent is looming ahead. Demographics are a major factor in this: in many Asian countries, the working population is aging, meaning there are too few talented people to replace those who retire. At the same time, downsizing has eliminated jobs but not work. Jobs are getting harder, people are working harder, vacations are being postponed, merit increases are being reduced, and people are unhappy. At the same time, the Internet has allowed people to market themselves like never before. Five years ago, online recruiter Monster had 20 million résumés worldwide—now it has 46 million. The combination of these factors will place talent management and retention firmly as top priorities for CHROs.

Proactive CHROs understand these priorities and HR's significant profit and loss (P&L) responsibility, a concept that many people struggle to comprehend. They focus on bringing in the right people and raising the bar for departments in an effective way. It's not enough for them to offer mere training and development programs; they need to focus on the company's objectives and realize when people are working out and when they are not. If a company gets HR right, and HR gets the right people in the right jobs, then the positive effectiveness of HR can be measured. Savvy line managers will be able to point at their results and show where HR made a difference.

Unfortunately, Asian companies tend to shy away from the more aggressive, proactive CHROs. They tend to dumb down the position and select HR people who are nice rather than effective, and to avoid people inclined to be pushy and ask questions, who can be among the most effective CHROs. Another mistake is simply not giving HR a spot at the top table.

While trust is earned, not given, companies must start somewhere. Companies must set expectations to ensure HR will be proactive and make a difference to the organization. One way Asian firms can start developing strong HR professionals is by giving their HR people a chance to work in other locations and experience other environments. This will give them the opportunity to learn from their global colleagues and peers. Unlike their counterparts in other departments, it is only rarely that Asian HR people have the opportunity to work abroad.

Perhaps most regrettable is the tendency in Asia to pay good HR people less than their true worth. The effective CHRO needs to be paid very well, but Asian companies often have the attitude that just because a person is top in HR, they should earn less than equivalent positions in other departments like finance, information technology (IT), and research and development (R&D). Top CHROs in the United States command packages in excess of US$1 million a year. A large government-linked company in Singapore recently hired its top HR executive for an unprecedented US$500,000 per year.

Generally, it is unwise to bring someone from another function into an HR role because outsiders only have experience with the tactical side of the role and don't have the fundamental HR disciplines and experiences to draw upon. They may underestimate the strategic talent management side of the role, and there is a real science to HR that they probably have never seen. The best HR people tend to come from conglomerates (as opposed to companies that focus on a specific niche) and tend to be Americans. Conglomerates tend to move HR people around and expose them to different businesses, allowing them to be challenged in different ways.

Moreover, top conglomerates treat the CHRO as part of their day-to-day business leadership team. Over the coming years, HR—and the role of the CHRO—will continue to evolve.

Beyond the Four P's: the Chief Marketing Officer

A new generation of marketing leaders has emerged. Guiding more than just the classic marketing mix, successful chief marketing officers (CMOs) are driving corporate strategy, holding general management responsibility, and developing next-generation talent in a function that was once relegated to the "four P's" of marketing (product, price, place and promotion). As the CMO role redefines itself across the business landscape, marketing leaders struggle to overcome functional stereotypes and prove their value to the organization.

That is especially true in Asia, points out Martin Roll, founder and CEO of VentureRepublic, a Singapore-based consultancy, and author of *Asian Brand Strategy: How Asia Builds Strong Brands*. "Most Asian businesses don't have a marketing representative at the senior management level, which is extremely important for Asian businesses to succeed," he told *The Edge Financial Daily* in Malaysia (June 6, 2008). There is a need to give marketing a boardroom-level position, he says. "[Having a CMO is] a very new concept in Asia—99 percent of all Asian businesses have no clear strategies when it comes to dealing with marketing on a more senior level, and it's a very big challenge for Asian businesses...

"CEOs orchestrate what companies should do—ranging from general management to leadership. CFOs work on the financial aspects—they're caretakers of a company's revenue—whereas CMOs generate the revenue. CMOs find new markets, new revenue streams, customers and loyalties—which are all functions of marketing," says Roll. "Especially in a congested marketplace with generic products, marketing and branding take centre stage—it's about using brands as an asset, and that's why it's important to have CMOs there."

The opportunities in Asia are profound, but so is the diversity of markets and media for communication. The difference between neighboring countries can be profound; for example, Japan has the greatest newspaper readership in the world (the *Yomiuri Shimbun* has about 16 million daily readers, compared to about 2 million for the *Wall Street Journal*). Across the Sea of Japan, however, South Korea boasts the most connected country in the world, with broadband Internet penetration rates of 90 percent.

"Asia has 2 billion consumers [who] drink our products relatively infrequently compared to other parts of the world. It's a huge opportunity with big populations, low category development, high economic growth, increasing affordability," Darren Marshall, Coca-Cola's group marketing director for the Pacific Group, told *Advertising Age* (May 19, 2008). "Asians have different languages, cultures, religions. But in most cases, consumer motivations are very, very similar. If we're going to create efficiencies, we need to work together. This is Asia, so everything is built on relationships. Rather than have 30 countries create 30 platforms in 30 unique ways, we have one country build a platform for the broader group. It also creates a sense of interdependence. For example, the Philippines has a "Coke with food" platform. Thailand has the development center focused on refreshment. The benefit of this structure is we're getting better work, faster, with less development cost."

In this new era, CMOs should be asking themselves: What is the proper role of marketing at my organization, and how can it be used to create as much value as possible? Great chief marketers who understand the importance of creating value for their companies must be great leaders who can generate trust and build connectivity throughout their organizations. Carlos Cata, principal of the CMO Practice at Heidrick & Struggles, says these skills are vital for new era of CMO:

- *Leadership:* Strong leadership is critical for CMOs who want to look past their own roles within the marketing function and to create value throughout their organizations. CMOs must move away from thinking like functional executives embedded in their own siloed departments, and instead think like operational executives.
- *Results:* Competence—a driver of trust—comes down to showing real results in the short term and long term. There has been a lot of

talk about "return on marketing investment," and that's certainly a critical measure of marketing's value and importance. Unfortunately, most CEOs simply don't have the patience to wait for returns that may not come for several years. Keep using such metrics, the better to build long-term equity for the marketing function. Go after quick wins as well, preferably through efforts worked on in close contact with individual business units.

- *Connectivity:* Great chief marketers must both understand the customer and make sure the customer's voice is heard at every level of the company, and evangelize marketing's value throughout the organization. Spend less time in focus groups and meeting with the advertising agency. Instead, spend time with the heads of every business unit. Visit the R&D department. Go out on sales calls.

Risky Business: Evolving Role of the Chief Risk Officer

The role of chief risk officer (CRO) has evolved since James Lam coined the term in the early 1990s, when he set up a new risk framework at GE Capital and gave himself the title of CRO. Previously seen as the preserve of the major financial institutions, the CRO role has increasingly been adopted by a wide range of industries.

Today's CRO commonly reports either directly or by dotted line to the chief executive officer, where previously the reporting line was to the chief financial officer or the chief operating officer. Even if the line to the CEO's office is not direct, the sponsorship from the top is clear. While risk management has been a technical role, with analytical skills being critical, it is now morphing into a business or strategy role—one requiring leadership and communication skills akin to the qualities normally seen in CEOs.

The CRO role is splitting into two distinct positions:

- The CRO as a genuine partner in business management, playing a critical role in growth strategy, product strategy, and mergers and acquisitions.
- The "chief compliance officer," shouldering the responsibility for corporate-level reporting, operational risk, and regulatory compliance. Regulations such as Sarbanes-Oxley, Basel II and a plethora of other standards have raised the workload to the point that a new senior position is necessary.

The CRO of Qantas Airways in Sydney, Rob Kella, sees his role as being enterprise-based, but more directly in the operational area than the financial or strategic risk spaces. "We rate risk in three buckets—strategic, operational and financial," he says. "Strategic risk decisions are up to the chief executive and his executive management team—I'm not in a position to tell them how to manage strategic risk, but I can help with the tools to identify, assess strategies, and manage the associated issues and exposures.

"On financial risk, that's the central role of the CFO, though I will look at what his group does and interrogate some of the processes the finance group uses to make decisions. But I'm not going to be there day in, day out validating his decisions (say, the hedging strategy used by the business to manage a variety of financial exposures including foreign exchange, interest rate, and key commodity price fluctuations). "It's in the operational area where I have a more direct role in terms of aviation safety, occupational health, security, environmental aspects, and enterprise risk from an audit perspective."

The Risk and Assurance Group at Qantas was transformed from an activity-intense group to more of an advisory and monitoring area. The group consists of people from several professions with skills in security and intelligence, flight operations, safety systems, public health, ergonomics, behavioral motivation and human factors, and various other specialist risk and audit areas. Kella describes the journey from "involvement" to "advisory" as being a challenging one, with the main task being to get line management more actively involved in risk management.

According to Kella, today's new breed of CRO needs to be numerate, with strong process skills and abilities to communicate across an enterprise. "You can't get away from the financial implications of whatever you do, so being on top of the numbers is crucial. Then you need to have a strategic orientation and the process skills to develop frameworks that go through the 'plan, do, check, react/re-plan' cycle that underpins risk management."

He adds, "In a risk role, you can easily be involved in everything—but obviously you can't, there are limits. You can't be the keeper of all the risks."

Helen Thornton, vice president of risk at BlueScope Steel, says the function of risk management has evolved from "insurance, safety, and legal" to a more holistic approach. "We define risk as anything that is going to prevent you from achieving your business plans," she says. "We link it back to individual businesses, business plans, and strategic plans to get that more strategic focus. You could have sales and marketing risk, treasury risks, human resources issues, as well as external market factors."

BlueScope's main challenge is to manage the volatility inherent in commodity markets. She says a risk executive needs these skills:

○ Intimate understanding of the business
○ Healthy curiosity
○ Good communication and listening skills

The problem with risk is that when you are managing it properly, you are invisible. CROs need to be proactive. There is a danger in an unrocked boat. People need to be aware across an organization of how to anticipate risk.

The role of CRO is spreading across the business world. While a CRO makes good sense for financial services and energy companies because their industries are highly regulated and must deal in volatile markets, other logical areas include pharmaceuticals, health care, telecommunications, and transportation. These industries have traditionally led the way through mandatory regulatory pressures, standards of compliance, and catastrophic risk exposure. However, the growing trend, irrespective of industry, is for companies with more than US$1 billion in revenue, a complex risk profile, and interdependent risk management activities to acknowledge the strategic importance of the CRO.

Inside the Mind: Chief Information Officer

At leading regional and global corporations, turnaround experts of a different kind have started to take the technology helm as transformed business processes become a competitive advantage—and even a matter of survival. Such transformational chief information officers (CIOs) are usually charged with leading cultural change to enable reengineering of business processes across the enterprise.

They typically have a strategic technology vision, as well as a deep understanding of the various businesses within the business—and of the competitive landscape outside the business. Frequently, these transformational executives have been brought into a company that feels blindsided by new technologies adopted by rivals. They may be seeking a competitive edge, entering new markets, or addressing technology problems.

But who are such transformational executives, how do they do it, and where can they be found? A common theme is that they are a curious breed that has had experience either in different businesses entirely or in different aspects of the same industry. In addition, successful transformers enjoy the confidence of their CEO and the support of their peers.

Former Westpac CIO Michael Coomer believes the qualities that make up a successful change leader are mostly innate and intuitive—but they can be bred within companies when CIOs have the ability to spot and nurture talent. At Westpac, for example, "there are people I've been mentoring over several years, and some are ready to step into the role now," Coomer says.

"Many organizations have tried to manufacture such executives by teaching business skills to technologists or vice versa. But they have usually failed," he says. "The ideal person is not a pure technologist or a pure businessperson. They are usually not stellar at business, so are not necessarily CEO material, but also not necessarily CIO material in the old sense of being an IT person."

Coomer consults on IT strategy and transformation outside of Westpac through informal networks, advisory boards, and committees, as well as by reading up to 80 e-mails a day on topics relating to the financial services industry. He likes a "line of sight" across the bank, as well as across competitors. He believes effective communication, integrity, and resilience are vital. Perceptions of a hidden agenda or politics must be avoided. "Change is inevitable, but you have to communicate softly, without arrogance," he says. "Yet there are times you need to dig your heels in and tell your managers you're not going to blink on this one. You can't falter at the first hurdle. If it was easy, we would have done it years ago!"

Senior Vice President Danny Dale of the Boston Consulting Group lists several attributes of transformational CIOs:

- Credibility with the CEO
- Superior communication skills
- Ability to look right across the business and into the future

The CIO and CEO "need to be joined at the head rather than the hip—of one mind," says Dale. He adds: "[CIOs] have to look at the enterprise, create a five-year horizon, and then ask, 'what innovations do we need to make now that in five years will be driving this business?'" Dale says the CIO is not a technology visionary in the dot-com sense, but rather is someone who delivers on a strategy. National Australia Bank CIO Michelle Tredenick agrees. "I don't like the word *visionary*," she says. "You need someone who has a clear understanding of where the business is moving, and how technology can assist. But you also want someone who challenges the status quo."

The future generation of CIOs will take on greater responsibility for the profitability of their business, as well as the creation of analytical models to understand the behavior of customers.

Former Citigroup CIO Donna Vinci says that with the changing role of the CIO, many businesses have introduced training to ensure technologists are "more rounded" in their business and leadership skills. "Technologists often find the business environment very interesting, and as they understand how the business works, they are able to see more applicability and outcomes that can be generated," says Vinci. But they must learn to get away from technical jargon and speak more like their business colleagues. "We found that really helped break down a lot of communication barriers and build bridges across the business."

Vinci says that IT executives should be people who are innovative. "But they must ensure that innovation is driven by a tangible business outcome and they must be able to adapt to change, to think up and across the organization, and to understand the competitive environment of the business. "You need to be able to blend with any style of team and business," she says, "and bring together excellent communication strengths with technical business acumen and analytical strengths."

Orderly Supply: The Dawn of the Chief Procurement Officer

Chief procurement officers (CPOs) will transform Asia's corporate landscape, but they must have support from top management.

Globalization also means that trends visible in the West over the last two decades have an accelerated effect in Asia. A good example of this is the dawning trend toward powerful CPOs. This trend has been apparent in the United States and Europe since the early 1990s. At big firms, a CPO is a strategic leader looking after an integrated supply chain and purchasing operation. In the truest sense, a CPO has a global perspective, coordinating the global purchasing of commodities and coordinating standardized contracts for items ranging from travel to heavy equipment. This powerful position first appeared in the United States, migrated to Europe, and will be seen increasingly in Asia.

The evidence is already here. In 2006, IBM announced its CPO, John Paterson, would move to Shenzhen, China. At the time of the announcement, the company said it employed more than 1,850 procurement and logistics staff in the region, and that spending in Asia accounted for about 30 percent of the company's US$40 billion annual procurement outlay. "We have a large customer and supply base in the US, in Europe and in Latin America," Paterson told the *Wall Street Journal* (October 12, 2006). "This will help us on a global basis, not just in the local market."

Other companies seem to share this point of view: the CPO of Canadian telecommunications giant Nortel is based in Hong Kong, and the CPO of semiconductor maker Freescale is based in Singapore. For Asia's procurement sector, the presence of such high-caliber executives in the region represents a major break from the past. In the 1980s, 1990s, and the early part of this decade, such executives were a rarity in Asia; the region was the purview of buyer specialists and buyer consolidators, scouting for cheap opportunities.

A powerful CPO entrenched in the highest echelons can drive dramatic change. Traditionally, the heroes of organizations have been found in sales and marketing, and such individuals traditionally made procurement decisions locally, an arrangement that often resulted in redundancy and higher costs. A CPO with a broad area of responsibility can be a powerful change evangelist across the organization, and able to make a difference to the bottom line from a very early stage.

Given the novelty of the CPO position in the region, entrenched interests in organizations will be skeptical, particularly if it means surrendering procurement powers. It is therefore essential that a new CPO make a mark within the first 100 days. The first place to have the necessary impact is in consolidating buying power; by doing so, a CPO gains an immense negotiating edge with vendors. This consolidation is easily done, and can show demonstrable savings early on. Following this, issues such as packaging and the consolidation of logistics suppliers offer substantial opportunities. After these early wins, CPOs can focus on the longer-term savings available in production processes.

Who's Guarding Your Data? The Chief Privacy Officer

When an Australian Internet service provider (ISP) had details of customers' credit cards published on the Internet by a hacker, it faced a serious crisis. Within months, the ISP was out of business. The fact that the computer thief got three years in jail was cold comfort for a company left with debts in the tens of millions of dollars.

Another high-profile privacy breach occurred when a Melbourne mobile phone company outsourced its transaction processing to India and then found that an employee of the offshore company was selling its customer lists. All the contractual obligations in the world can't stop an inside job. Some examples are embarrassing rather than financially disastrous, such as the recent accidental publication by the NSW police force of the passwords of senior counterterrorism officers and hundreds of journalists who signed up to receive information from its media unit.

Whether privacy breaches are caused by disgruntled or inept employees or deliberate outside attacks, today's reality is that information is a keenly sought and often vulnerable asset. Privacy management is complicated by widely differing legislative frameworks. In Australia, for example, state legislation—particularly around health information—was written in the late 1980s and early 1990s, before computer databases were aggregated.

Faced with the consequences of financial loss and damage to reputation from privacy breaches, more companies have responded by appointing expert compliance and privacy officers. Often, the appointee has a strong legal background and is familiar with all aspects of compliance. The chief privacy officer must possess the same qualities of leadership and business acumen that boards and CEOs expect of other C-level executives.

Privacy executives must be proactive: The chief privacy officer needs to be aware of legal requirements to ensure compliance, but must also be able to spot trends and put in place measures to protect against emerging issues. We see privacy not just as a tactical matter but also as a strategic issue. By leading the way in privacy protection, businesses can enhance their reputations with customers and consumers, and ultimately grow market share. As the Australian federal privacy commissioner, Karen Curtis, told a conference in New Zealand recently, "good privacy is good business."

Privacy Commissioner Curtis says legal training helps privacy officers—"but it's more important that the person is senior enough to have access to the board or a board committee." Curtis says that high-level access is the best way to ensure a business is complying with privacy laws—"You need to embed it into business practice and into the culture."

Privacy expert Philip Argy, formerly with law firm Mallesons Stephen Jaques, offers the humorous-but-serious scenario of a possible future Orwellian world where a customer phones a fast-food outlet to order a pizza, only to be told that their unique identifier number has been matched to a medical database revealing the customer has high cholesterol. "The operator says that in order to safeguard his company from a lawsuit, he must suggest the customer does not have pizza."

Another major issue today, according to Argy, is that of identity theft. If a business holds any personal information about an individual, it essentially commits a criminal offense by refusing to let that person access it. "Since most requests for that information are made by phone," adds Argy, "your dilemma now is: 'How do I know if you are who you say you are?' You would ask for the mother's maiden name, date of birth, and a few other items—which is very weak protection, considering you're literally criminally damned if you do and damned if you don't."

Argy says the best protection for a business is to have an extremely competent person at a senior level with responsibility for privacy and compliance across every facet of the business. "What I would not advocate is a chief privacy officer as a separate area. I don't like silos for anything, but in this area in particular, you want someone who is in charge of what is, in effect, a continuum of compliance responsibilities.

"The role of what is really data protection involves a broad range of skills and knowledge. It may draw on people from many backgrounds, including law, government affairs, technology, auditing, or intelligence."

From Multinational Corporation to Private Equity Executive

When Blackstone announced the appointment of former Hong Kong Financial Secretary Antony Leung as a senior managing director and chairman of its Greater China operations in January 2007, it marked another milestone in an ongoing trend of Asia's high-profile executives defecting to private equity (PE) firms.

The world's largest players have been adding dots on their corporate maps denoting offices in Hong Kong, Japan, Singapore, or India, and courting Asia's top executives (who often join as operating partners)—some with the view to eventually running a major portfolio company. In April 2007 for example, Michelle Guthrie, former Asia CEO of STAR Television, joined Providence Equity Partners as managing director, and the Carlyle Group scooped up Patrick Siewert and Herman Chang as senior directors. Siewert's last position was Coca-Cola's president and chief operating officer for East, South Asia & Pacific Rim, while Chang was Delphi's president for China and managing director for the Asia Pacific operations of a global product business unit.

While this may seem to attest to the allure of senior roles in PE, "this industry is not for everyone," as Chang, now at Carlyle, points out. Jim Tsao agrees. Tsao joined CCMP Capital Asia in 2005, leaving behind the group managing director role at one of the largest listed food products companies in Hong Kong—a role he held for eight years. "It was my dream to become the CEO of a listed company since my business school days, and I achieved that at the age of 40," he says. "I had turned around a company that was at the brink of bankruptcy and helped reestablish it as the regional industry leader in its core segment. However, my learning curve was flattening out, as things went from hectic to organized, and then to routine. It was way too early for me to think about retirement and I was looking to take up another challenge. I felt that joining a PE firm would give me the chance to get back onto a steep learning curve, and to see different industries and geographies that I had not seen before. The opportunity to feel excited again was the biggest kick!

"That excitement has lasted till today, two years into the job change—but one must understand that things are very different in this environment. You are no longer surrounded by troops of subordinates who take orders from you. You are likely to be surrounded by a team of young professionals who challenge things from all directions. For me personally, the transition from being one of the youngest CEOs of a listed company to being one of the most senior members of the team took some adjustment."

Of the transition to private equity (PE), "You have to be ready for the role change," Tsao says. "A CEO is like the captain of a football team. You enjoy the game and putting together your team—and get to play the game yourself passionately. In PE, your role is like that of the owner of the sports club. You need to find out what game is popular and which club is a good investment. Then you need to find the team that can play to win, and finally, find a good buyer after you have lifted the status of the club. You now have a much broader view in the sports arena and you will get to see a lot more games and players. But as you are no longer a player, there will be times you miss the action."

The role of owner clearly requires a broader perspective of long-term opportunities, threats, market trends, potential buyers, and exit plans. "At any multinational or a PE portfolio company, the focus is on delivering results. The journey there, however, looks quite different," says Siewert, now at Carlyle. "In PE, the vision, goals, and deliverables are very clear; communication between strategic PE investors and management is also far more transparent, open, and supportive. In a public company with numerous stakeholders and prerequisite disclosure protocols, communication tends to be more guarded."

3

GETTING TO THE TOP: LEADERSHIP DEVELOPMENT

The leadership qualities required to reach the C-level are the subject of endless debate. The media focus on "strategies for success," as if following a 10-step program can get you into the corner office. Meanwhile, tales of ruthlessness abound in modern fiction, portraying an image of power-hungry people clawing their way to the top.

Nothing could be further from the truth. Not only is the degree of humility required greatly underestimated, but the standout characteristic—an innate ability to get along with potential competitors—is overlooked as a critical success factor.

"People skills" can mean the ability to influence people and enjoy the company of others. But it also means the ability to fuse a team together and get everyone moving in the right direction rather than just removing problematic individuals and replacing them with more compliant ones. "Hard work" is a given, as many chief executive officers, chief information officers, and chief financial officers will testify. Of course, you really have to want the job.

From interviews with several top executives around the region, here are some of the "must-have" leadership qualities that emerge:

- Total commitment to the role—you have to want it, and you have to be married to it (to put it first in your life)
- Communication skills—particularly listening, influencing, and negotiating
- Congeniality—the ability to build relationships with people you might otherwise detest

- Consultative character—allowing others to help you solve problems

Do you really want it?

BHP Billiton former CIO Dave Richardson says it is important for aspiring executives to ask themselves whether the top job is for them. "If it is what you want, you need to be honest enough with yourself about whether you've got what it takes and whether you are prepared to make the sacrifices necessary to get the top job. Everybody works hard these days, but there is a real commitment to this sort of role."

Richardson, who has had senior IT roles in a range of industries, from retailing with Myer and Coles Myer, banking with ANZ, and airlines with both Ansett and Singapore Airlines, says a key success factor for executives is the ability to get up to speed reasonably quickly on the critical areas of the role—working out what's different and what stays the same. "That doesn't mean that I need to be an in-depth expert on everything about the business," Richardson says. "But I do have to understand the business, understand what the key drivers are, as well as the operational issues and opportunities. You need to work out what the real levers are and what's really important, as opposed to what's 'nice to know.'"

He says the way executives earn their pay over a year is by carrying the load of half a dozen major decisions, while "the other stuff is done and executed through people."

The critical characteristic is to be a people person, Richardson says. "You are only truly successful through other people. You can have the best ideas in the world, the best strategy, the best judgment, and the best experience. But things are going to get done through others."

He says that if an executive does not have a real interest in helping to develop the careers of others, developing their skills and helping them communicate well, "then you're picking the wrong career and the wrong aspiration." Being able to work with people you may not necessarily like is also an essential ingredient in the mix, according to Richardson. "It's important to have people around you and reporting to you, who in many ways are quite different from you and how you think, and they may go about doing things in a way you wouldn't do," he says.

Three Steps to Success

Michael Coomer, former group executive for business and technology solutions and services at Westpac, says three main factors enable a C-level executive to be successful:

- The quality of the people the executive appoints to surrounding positions
- The quality of those the executive chooses to work with
- The quality of the decision making that follows

"You might be the best decision maker in the world, but if you are not surrounded by the right people who can either execute or support the decisions inside the business, then your decisions are meaningless," he says. "It's all about getting that combination of the right people who are working for you, and then I think you can back your judgment."

In building relationships with diverse personalities, Coomer says he focuses on capability rather than personality. "Invariably, you will be confronted with the issue of having people around you who make you feel very uncomfortable—and they make you feel uncomfortable because they challenge your own judgment. But provided their values are aligned and their motivations are aligned, you can cope with any of those issues well. However, the moment you believe their motives and values are not aligned culturally, then that's time to part company."

Another key is networks—internal and external, formal and informal—Coomer says. Keeping in touch with a wide range of people in the IT industry enables him to keep up with trends. "You also literally absorb as much information as you possibly can. While accounting standards might be changed on a generational basis, IT standards change every day. You can't keep abreast of that by sitting behind your desk, so there's quite a lot of travel involved. One of the reasons for the high turnover of C-level and CIOs is that 'wear-out' factor."

Critical Capabilities

Edward Nicol, director of information management and CIO at Cathay Pacific Airways, says the two critical capabilities for successful leadership are getting along with people and getting things done. He elaborates on these factors:

"'Getting along with people' is not just about being liked and loved; it is about being able to understand people and to discern what drives them, how they view things, and being able to influence them in a collaborative way. It's about people management." The term "people management" also includes clarity of communication, negotiating skills, influencing skills, and the ability to partner with internal and external stakeholders.

The ability to get things done is critical. "You have to make a difference. People should notice that something happens when you are there that would not happen if you weren't." Nicol adds, "If you can't answer the question, 'What do you contribute in your job?' you have a big problem."

A standout quality is an executive's ability to identify opportunities and to come up with a solution where none apparently exists. "You don't employ a C-level to keep things ticking over, but to make a difference, to get something done—to dramatically grow sales, profits, or make acquisitions, or whatever. In our case, for example, it could be not just about getting the airline menus out on time but about being innovative on menus or meal concepts, or the structure of the contracts with the suppliers, or how to deliver the in-flight service in the kitchen."

Canadian-born former Coles Myer CIO Peter Mahler says that while intellectual capability is essential in an executive, "the primary thing" is the work ethic. "I could easily have come to Australia and worked in consulting in telco or airlines, but instead, I went into something totally new. I had to do my homework at nights as well as my day job, to learn about the industry. I went out into stores and asked others who'd been in retail 20 or 30 years if they had the time to help me learn. And I must say they did. Look, if your day job is a 60-hour job, you still have at least weekends to learn the new technology or the new business."

Mahler believes in being consultative. His Mondays are usually completely blocked off—he spends time with leaders of all the big projects, and the layer beneath those leaders. "We have meetings from morning to dusk and I have these people coming at me from every level. It's time for them to spend with their CIO and bounce things off me and tell me their problems. That way, I get a complete picture from the ground up." He says it is not easy for executives to work with those who may have incompatible personalities—"but you just cannot let personalities get in the way. You have to take emotions out of the equation. You have to look beyond their foibles and seek out their capabilities. They got to where they are for a reason." Mahler says the "people compatibility issue" trips up most potential leaders at the middle management layer.

He believes attention to detail is vital. "You see the big picture but check that your goals are being achieved," he says. "You can't delegate that. You have to have a real love affair with the job and be very involved."

Breaking Through to Senior Management

It is not technical skills or education that set senior leaders apart, it is their finely honed relationship skills. One client, a powerful banking CEO who was six months into his new job, remarked, "I miss banking. It's all about people."

Competent, highly qualified people fill the cubicles and offices of Asia's corporations. Executives with MBAs and advanced degrees in key business disciplines are common, as are ambitious people with years of experience under their belt. But for all the qualifications, skills, and experience many possess, only a special few manage to break free from the ranks of middle management and into truly pivotal senior roles.

On the surface, the attributes of a top executive are readily apparent and (in theory) easily replicated. Top managers often have extensive education and years of experience. This includes time spent outside their home country, as overseas experience is increasingly crucial in today's globalized world. But there is substantially more to being a successful senior manager than can be listed on a résumé.

"A successful executive must be able to create a shared vision and mission," says Chris Chua, Malaysia country head for pharmaceutical company Janssen-Cilag. "He should be able to recognize and recruit the right people, be a good communicator and motivator, and be able to capture people's hearts, minds, and imagination." The qualities Chua cites are essential in the complex organizations of today, but candidates often prefer hierarchical environments where they can work smoothly through direct reports, and few organizations today are this simple.

The skill to influence others is especially crucial in companies with a matrix structure, which are often ambiguous environments where executives have more than one boss and several direct reports. To be successful in such an organization, one must understand different personalities and interrelationships between personalities, and work with them to get results.

While decisiveness is a classic attribute of leaders throughout history, in the corporate environment, the ability to explain decisions is just as important as the ability to make them. Senior leaders are accountable to a range of stakeholders—the board, shareholders, employees, and the media—and must possess the people skills to influence all of them.

Koh Phee Wah, former head of Southeast Asia for medical device maker Becton, Dickinson, and Company, says it is assumed that a senior executive has superb communication skills, coupled with the ability to adjust styles in various countries. "These are not skills taught in a classroom, and a lot of it is personal judgment," he says.

Successful executives need to learn the environment in which the company operates. Once they've done this, they need to master complex business problems, lead visionary change, get the entire management team involved, and finally execute for results. Just one of these responsibilities, getting the management team involved, requires many different skills, including communicating and building relationships and developing people and teams.

Cultural Awareness Is Key

Aside from people skills, understanding and shaping a company's culture is key for breaking through to senior management. Those who move from company to company throughout their career will need to be acutely sensitive to the nuances of a new employer—even companies in the same industry can have radically different cultures, as at PC makers Dell and Toshiba. Understanding corporate culture is essential if one is to influence the right people and get things done. When new CEOs without this cultural sensitivity try to make radical change, they often fail and exit the organization.

Aside from being highly observant, one way to learn a new corporate culture quickly is to find a mentor. A supportive mentor can be a great asset, but it is important that the aspiring senior executive demonstrate self-direction and independence. It is worth noting that many senior executives can point to a few key mentors in their careers. Freddie Laker, mentor to Virgin Atlantic's Richard Branson, once told Branson: "Make a fool of yourself. Otherwise you won't survive." A mentor to Warren Buffett once told him: "You're right not because others agree with you but because your facts are right."[1]

However valuable soft skills may be, it all may be in vain if no one notices. Aspiring senior executives need to take the initiative by volunteering to take on projects—and then perform exceptionally well. Ideally, try to cross boundaries. For example, a person working in one discipline, such as finance, should try to take on projects in other disciplines, such as human resources or marketing. This will make it possible to gain experience in a range of key areas, build a network throughout the organization, and ultimately build a prominent profile. But choose projects carefully. The best projects are those that are achievable and have quantifiable, measurable results.

Janssen-Cilag's Chua notes that Asian executives are seldom as vocal and articulate as their Western counterparts. "They are often not as assertive; they have a tendency to be overrespectful of authority," he says. "Often, they are perceived as technocrats. They get the job done, but they may not be perceived as leadership material."

Chua adds, "For an Asian executive to be successful, he must not only win the trust of his constituents, but also earn the trust and confidence of headquarters. In other words, he must also be capable of thinking and behaving like a Westerner. Because of this, it is not surprising that many Asians who make it to senior management roles often have an MBA from a prestigious Western university and some work experience in the West."

What Makes a Leader in a Flat World?

How well are executives learning to be global citizens? Can they stand alone in foreign environments far from their support systems, make decisions, and take actions that work?

The fundamental qualities of leadership have not changed in centuries. Good leaders then as now had vision, strove to do something different, and distinguished themselves by outstanding abilities of some kind. What has changed is the knowledge that leaders must possess—and the need to refresh that knowledge constantly to face changing circumstances. This focuses attention on the shelf life of leadership, and on the need for leaders and organizations to plan renewal into their lives.

Recent business theory and history demonstrates the need to develop planning for the next life cycle while the current one is at its height. The principle holds as much for the individual as it does for the organization: both have to strive for continual development.

But the fundamental attributes of leadership remain the same:

- Trustworthiness, fairness and unassuming behavior
- Sensitivity to people and situations

- Flexibility and adaptability
- The capacity to make sound and timely decisions

To that list must now be added the ability to immerse oneself in a new culture and work hard to understand it, without falling into the trap of judging it. Search firms looking for leaders are reaching beyond superficial judgments on the basis of work history.

Historically, checking references with a superior was routine. Today, search firms take a more comprehensive approach. Recruiters talk to peers and subordinates as well as superiors, closing in on specifics such as these:

- How does this person go about building a team?
- Was this person effective—how, specifically?
- What results were achieved?
- What is this person's management style?

The outcome of a search is to identify and place in a C-suite role someone who is an independent thinker, and who is prepared to nurture a team—and accept the final responsibility of leadership.

Transparency equals no place to hide. Greater transparency in organizations has profound implications for leaders and for the selection of people who will be effective leaders. Transparency is also widening the gap between leaders and managers. Flatter structures tend to sharpen the edge of individual responsibility. Roles are less blurred. Wider information sharing across intra- and extracompany networks leaves less opportunity for "information politics" or the old "knowledge is power and I'm going to hoard it" mentality. People can communicate sideways more easily without going through a hierarchy.

For the top team, these changes mean less involvement with transferring knowledge and more involvement in the development of leadership and team-building skills.

Commitment to Asia

Asia is a great place for a career, but there are many misperceptions about Asia's hiring market, and landing a role requires a major commitment.

Every year, Asia's executive search firms receive thousands of unsolicited e-mails from Europeans and Americans seeking roles in

Asia. These hopefuls come from a range of backgrounds, from freshly minted MBAs to managers who see a stint in Asia as something to enhance their résumé. The one thing all have in common is an awareness of Asia's extraordinary growth story, and a desire to participate in this growth.

Unfortunately, this flood of correspondence betrays many common misperceptions about Asia and the realities of the region's job market. Perhaps the biggest misperception is about the shortage of talent in Asia. Yes, Asia has a shortage of skilled managers, but companies operating in the region have a strong preference for hiring managers locally: local managers understand their markets, speak the language, and have top-notch educational credentials often earned at quality schools in the West. While Asia may have severe shortages in some highly specialized fields that can only be filled by specialists from the West, plenty of Asian generalists are available to work as managers in key functional areas such as finance and marketing.

Many Westerners also fail to understand the sophistication of modern Asia. In the 1980s and 1990s, multinationals viewed Asia as an area for low-cost manufacturing. Ambitious managers in the United States and Europe saw the region as something of a corporate backwater, a good place to spend a few years, perhaps, but a bad place to advance one's career. Globalization and the rise of vast consumer economies in the region have changed this. Increasingly, board-level executives from major Western companies are relocating to the region, with the result that the caliber of executive talent one finds in Asia Pacific is as good as one finds in Europe and the United States.

Many seeking jobs in Asia completely overestimate their chances of winning the famed "expat package." There was a time when a manager transferred to Asia could count on a range of perks: an apartment, a car (with driver), school for the kids, club memberships and business class tickets home every year for the entire family. While such packages still exist, they are far less common, and all but impossible to land for somebody who is not a senior executive transferring to Asia within the same company. Even executives with expat packages have discovered their entitlements are only good for a few years, and find themselves put on local terms should they decide to stay in the region.

It is possible to move one's career in Asia, but the most important prerequisite is profound commitment to Asia. Assuming the region is in desperate need of talent, many executives who seek to work there openly state they want to spend a few years in Asia before returning home. This apparent lack of commitment is anathema for employers, who only want to invest in individuals who are committed to Asia for the long haul. Starting a career in Asia must be viewed as one of life's most important decisions, and thus given the appropriate amount of thought. Only this level of commitment will make an impression on possible employers.

For those seeking a transfer to Asia, there are a number of ways to show this commitment. Learning an Asian language such as Mandarin at your own expense is very useful. For executives whose current role does not offer the opportunity of business trips to the region, it is advisable to visit it, again at personal expense. Such trips demonstrate interest in Asia while providing opportunities to build relationships and grasp the challenges the company faces in the region. Executives can also show their interest in Asia by getting involved in projects that focus on the region, which provide exposure to Asia and possibly the chance to travel there. If these approaches fail, remaining options include joining another company that has operations in Asia, or perhaps moving to the region to search for a job.

Another route to Asia is through the MBA schools operating in the region. In Singapore, one finds both INSEAD and the Chicago School of Business; in Manila, there is the Asian Institute of Management; and the MBA programs at Hong Kong's universities are well regarded. Earning an MBA in the region offers the opportunity to get a hands-on feel of the market and build a network of contacts, all of which can be invaluable when conducting a job search.

Finally, those coming to Asia with little work experience in the region must be willing to make sacrifices in regard to their compensation. While this may be painful in the short term, it should be seen as an opportunity to score some successes, prove your credentials in the Asian context, and open the door to further career advancement in the region.

What has emerged from a 2005 Heidrick & Struggles survey is that the predictors for success in these roles are not necessarily those traditionally assumed. Interestingly, the mold for a successful executive is rather malleable; extensive experiences in a particular Asian country, an understanding of the culture, or even the ability to speak a local language are not the most important factors. What then is the most effective predictor for success in this role? *Adaptability and cultural inquisitiveness*. The right attitude is critical. Successful employees have a respect for the culture and sensitivity to its differences, if not a complete understanding.

A typical example is that of a European regional manager who decorated his house in the local style after moving from Korea to India to be a better host to his guests. Another is a managing director who did not speak any Asian language fluently—but could belt out an assortment of karaoke favorites.

People such as these are adaptable to different cultures; they may not do so perfectly every time, but they are observant and able to make changes (for example, in their communications style). Another facet of—or perhaps requirement for—this ability is a sense of humility: the understanding that you do not know all but are willing to learn.

Paul W. Bradley, former managing director of IDS Logistics International, points out that cultural awareness at least can be taught. Office layouts can be changed and employees can be transferred to different countries, placed with people of different cultural backgrounds, or encouraged to interact through social events.

Still, successful leaders are able to transcend culture. In the words of David N. Edwards, former managing director of Johnson & Johnson Vision Care Asia Pacific, "great leaders will be followed in any country... great leaders will find a way to get it done."

Key things when considering moving to a career in Asia:

- Asia is no longer a corporate backwater; the executive talent in the region rivals that found in developed markets.
- Expat packages are increasingly uncommon; many Westerners with careers in the region are now on local packages.
- To land a role, it is key to demonstrate a firm commitment to a long-term career in the region.
- It is best to knock on company doors directly; executive search firms focus on the needs of their clients, who seek executives with experience in the region.

Are Your Executives On Board or Overboard?

A recent Australian example of poor on-boarding at the CEO level saw the parachute costs running into several million dollars, lost revenue into the tens of millions—and the loss of several key executives destabilized by the process.

While a smokescreen of divergent versions of events helped to contain the reputation damage, the experience is not uncommon.

Although precise numbers are hard to pin down, Heidrick & Struggles estimates that the success rate of senior executives over a two-year period is less than 40 percent. This is in businesses where incoming executives have a clearly defined mandate and recruitment processes.

This failure rate is increasing as businesses scramble and often compromise in the search for talent in an increasingly competitive and globalized marketplace. Some 728 chief executives left their jobs in the United States in the first half of 2006, some by choice, but most unwillingly.

Why are newly recruited senior executives failing? Often, there is a lack of time and effort in the initial integration of the new executive. In discussions with senior executives at one major Australian corporation—over an incident where the CEO was well-qualified, yet fumbled the ball—several mistakes were identified:

- Failed to build relationships with the board
- Brought in new team members who did not understand the business
- Did not consult widely enough, and when he did, failed to share the results of his findings with those who could have helped him execute a turnaround plan

While the new chief executive had introduced a major cost-cutting plan and planned a merger to ensure ongoing profitability in a competitive sector, he did not deliver on the plan and in fact was gone within six months.

Overcome Style Issues

An interesting comment was that the executive was "too autocratic" in style. Yet this style issue could have been overcome with proper onboarding, giving the newcomer an understanding of the collegiate culture he was entering. "He made a fundamental mistake which could easily have been rectified," says a senior executive who worked with the new CEO. "If he'd been more transparent, instead of hoarding the information he was uncovering as he investigated the issues—not to mention the plan he was preparing for change—his top team would have given him feedback, and helped him to execute a slightly modified proposal."

As it was, the new leader started to implement change without support and a bitter battle ensued, resulting in his departure.

The importance of the first few months of a new executive's administration has been identified by numerous leadership experts, including Michael Watkins, former management professor at the INSEAD business school and author of the *First 90 Days* series of books aimed at leaders of all levels.

Deloitte Touche Tohmatsu's People and Performance partner Alec Bashinsky says the pressure is on Australian boards to deliver short-term value to shareholders. "While leaders brought in as change agents can usually align the business to the new goals within six months, the cultural aspects of transformation can take up to 10 years. There can be a major push to get the share price up, but the program should also be to achieve cultural change and alignment of financial reporting, and that's not something you can achieve overnight," he says. "One individual can't do it, so you need a person who is able to forge a team who will do it with him. They need to be contractually set up in terms of a parachute. If anything goes wrong, that's potentially a 10-year break in their career."

Bashinsky says the on-boarding process usually takes place while the executive is in transition from a preceding role. He gives the example of a C-level executive who was moving from one bank to another, who took three months "gardening leave," using this time to read up and understand strategy, meet his new CEO and executive team, and gain a deep understanding of the new corporate structure and values.

"Now, even though you're not supposed to do that, there is usually some opportunity for the (C-level executive) coming in to be able to do some of that background work so they hit the ground running. If you leave it until day one, you're going to be struggling to get yourself up and running in the first 30 days," he says.

"Information immersion" is critical. Bashinsky says that if the board can supply business plans, strategy data, and a clear map of the organization's structure, the C-level executive comes aboard with a good understanding of the territory.

"I know of one individual who was brought on from a like-minded IT organization but was not given much detail. When he started to meet with the business players, they suddenly realized the job fit was not there. This created angst and it ended up getting into quite an antagonistic debate. The individual ended up separating after about two months because of that lack of transparency."

AMP CIO Lee Barnett says that the keys for an executive getting a fast start in a new role are:

- Determining what success will look like for the board and the CEO
- Getting the best people on board to make it happen

She says the top priorities for incoming executives are getting their team in place—"You can't do much until you've done that"—and sorting and organizing the available people to ensure they are building the capabilities that will help take the company forward.

SingTel Group CIO Ng Yoke Weng agrees that the on-boarding process should start long before the executive joins, to avoid mismatches between expectations and reality. "Sometimes the job description doesn't really fully represent the nature of the job—the role may be more about the intangibles in the culture and the working relationships," Ng says.

"In my case, because I moved from one large corporation to another, the transition was very smooth. But if you come from a small to medium business or from running your own business, some adjustments will be needed—mainly in the area of governance. [Incoming executives] may have been led to expect considerable latitude, but when they join, they don't have as much latitude as they thought. This may mean that their style isn't suited to that culture."

Ng says incoming executives need to talk to those who have worked for the company, or served it in a vendor capacity, as well as to key people in the new company. "You need to get an external view, and then talk to existing executives. You need to know even small things such as whether the senior executives call each other by first names or have to address each other as 'Mr.'—this will give you some inkling of what you could be facing."

Nine Steps to On-Boarding

The on-boarding of senior executives should not be left to chance. An investment in on-boarding is arguably as important as the investment in recruitment. Bob Chrismer and Michael Thompson of Heidrick & Struggles have identified nine key steps to securing a headache-free on-boarding process:

1. Start on-boarding during recruitment, ensuring a staged schedule of contacts between the candidate and the company.
2. Designate an appropriate mentor who will help the newcomer build a strong network within the senior levels.
3. Show the incoming executive exactly how to get things done in the new environment.
4. Tailor the on-boarding program to the individual, taking into account the newcomer's strengths and weaknesses and areas that will need critical support in the coming months.
5. Define deliverables covering the first 60 and 120 days, the first six months and first year, so the executive can drive revenue while assimilating the new culture.
6. Get the executive on a project team—any team. The fastest way to get a new executive moving is by total immersion.
7. Integrate the executive into the peer group, seeking out those with mutual interests as well as recent arrivals.
8. Provide regular, constructive feedback.
9. Intervene early and often. Timely corrective action is important. Take a 360-degree "pulse check" with the new executive, the team, and peers to work out what is going well and what is not. Discuss ways to remove roadblocks and adjust resources to encourage success and prevent derailment. Convey successes widely and communicate a company-wide "buzz" around the achievements of the new executive.

With the accelerating pace of talent acquisition, a strong on-boarding program can be a formidable weapon and point of differentiation in any company that sees leadership talent as a source of competitive advantage.

Endnote

1 "The Big Interview: Sir Alan Sugar—The Lone Wolf Who Leads The Pack," 42 degrees, Bank of Scotland, July 2005. http://42degrees.bankofscotland.co.uk/issue-1/interview-2.html

II
LEADING OTHERS

4

BUILDING AND KEEPING TEAMS

The growth rate of many companies in the Asia Pacific region necessitates a multi-strategy hiring plan, with simultaneous recruiting over different levels of positions in addition to filling positions organically and through the poaching of talent.

Human resources departments of multinational corporations are succeeding in establishing or growing their presence in Asia. The staggering growth and further potential of the region cannot escape the notice of any company with a global vision. Given this situation, the demand for qualified, talented, and effective executives has outpaced the supply.

While the many professionals we consulted generally agree that corporate Asia is still developing in areas such as governance, HR practices, and entrepreneurial spirit, it is obvious that this situation is rapidly evolving.

An important example is the HR function in the region as described by one HR executive: "[It is] not seen as a place to work if you are interested in strategy, it is still a place to work if you're interested in administration." This situation possibly developed due to the hiring practices of the first multinationals locating in Asia. Companies came here for the cheap labor and adopted a "hire and fire" policy with no significant investment in talent.

Companies that are able to quickly and effectively elevate HR into a strategic role will have an advantage over their competitors. Companies that are not successful at this, or are slow off the mark, run the risk of losing out on talent in the long run. Poor HR infrastructure or practices such as vacancy-driven hiring can lead to a vicious cycle, whereby it becomes increasingly difficult to recruit high-level talent.

This leads to the question of what kind of talented employee is in high demand. Based on the results of a 2005 survey by Heidrick & Struggles, the demand is greatest for positions of senior leadership (such as general manager, CEO, or president). Because the skills required of these positions are much harder to define than those required of functional roles such as IT or finance, these top positions are much more difficult to fill.

Succession Strategies

On the day Carmel Gray announced her retirement as CIO of the Australian financial services company Suncorp, her successor was announced.

He was an internal candidate. He had good experience and came from a strong pool of credible candidates, all of whom had been screened and nurtured by CEO John Mulcahy.

Suncorp had also conducted a search to help benchmark the strongest internal candidates.

Done properly, succession planning can not only guarantee a corporation's fitness for the future and avoid costly disruption in an age of constant change, it can also build a culture of stability and talent retention.

According to Gray, the secret to her painless executive transition was constant scanning of the pool for potential leaders. "The top team met frequently for the purpose of reviewing the succession program," she says. "We discussed the progress of potential leaders and their development needs—for example, job rotation, mentoring, special training, and other strategies were tailored to each individual.

"Their managers had to learn to take risks and make short-term sacrifices in the longer-term interests of the company." Gray says that managers were made accountable for the results of the program and encouraged to develop a strategic focus on the company's business.

MBF Australia CIO Warwick Foster, formerly global CIO for Prudential and CIO of AMP, says the key to succession is to build a good team. "You can waste a lot of time if you don't focus on your people," he says. "I usually start with the basics—go through the titles and functions, the grading and the training, capability frameworks and career planning programs. Then I will merge the more generic functions and work through the competencies."

Foster says it is difficult in times of constant change to maintain a steady succession model—the world is changing too fast, with frequent reorganization and acquisition or divestment. "But if you have a strong team under you, it's easy to build up obvious successors. You're looking for people who are doing extracurricular activities beyond their day-to-day work, and who have three main areas of expertise—operational, technical, and strategic business linkage skills."

Foster admits it is not always possible to find candidates with all three competencies. If one competency is poorly developed, he says that it is more desirable to develop people who have a good IT understanding rather than those with pure business skills and little IT understanding. "We tried a non-IT specialist once in the UK and it didn't work. You really do need someone who has run a technology shop, and understands the technical direction and how that can then help the business achieve its goals. They need to have some experience in infrastructure and IT architectures."

Railcorp CIO Vicki Coleman agrees with Gray that a good succession plan needs to be in place before a CIO moves on. Before leaving her previous role with Sydney Water, Coleman put together a high-level plan, which involved first hiring an interim CIO and then conducting a search for her replacement.

"However, it is not appropriate to leave without having put a plan in place or taking steps to ensure there is a smooth handover."

Coleman says that at Sydney Water, she had a good senior management team, and they were all working on projects that were mission-critical to the business. "To disrupt any of the projects and ask one of them to fill my position in a caretaker role would not have been beneficial to the organization as a whole." Coleman had also tried to time her departure at a logical break. An interim executive was appointed and was able to finish ongoing projects ahead of the new CIO coming in while starting to plan the next steps of the evolving organization.

Good succession planning is not solely about how you replace your star performers. Your employees should not be blindsided when a leader is poached by a rival. The continuing downsizing of middle management and the shifting moods of a jittery workplace have complicated this issue and increased its impact on the culture of many companies. Many companies do not implement succession planning in a transparent manner. Their strategy is opaque and often causes unnecessary disruption, concern, and instability.

Effective succession planning requires at least five steps:

1. Identify future leaders.
2. Assess the talent against current and emerging needs.

3. Address their development needs by training, job rotation, or mentoring and coaching.
4. Monitor candidate progress.
5. Constantly benchmark candidates against potential external hires.

The way companies deal with succession depends on their size, and on the number and quality of candidates. Succession challenges will inevitably arise. It is better to be prepared than be forced into reactive mode. Organizations that develop credible successors will continue to attract the more loyal, talented, and ambitious executives.

Outside or Inside? Internal Versus External Hiring

The decision to promote from within or outside a company should never be black or white.

Is it better to hire from within or outside of your organization?

That is precisely the question that Heidrick & Struggles faced in 2006 when our then-chairman and CEO Tom Friel shared with the board his decision to step down as CEO. The firm had strong internal candidates, but was adamant about entertaining outside talent for Friel's successor. After a few months, the board met to review a short list of external candidates, but despite the exhaustive process, chose an internal applicant. While some may argue that we could have saved time and money by only looking within, the process ensured that every possible option was considered, and that we arrived at the best solution for the firm.

A large multinational in Asia faced a similar situation a few years back when its regional president left the company. Two candidates were in the wings internally, but neither was a true fit for the role. The company asked for Heidrick & Struggles' help on possible candidates and the skills they needed to possess to be successful. The organization, however, wanted to announce a decision quickly, and while neither internal candidate was ideal, they settled on one for the top job.

Disaster loomed from day one. Although the new president had sound technical skills and was familiar with the company, he quickly proved that he was unable to develop and drive strategy from the top. He was also too hands-on and incapable of delegating effectively. He soon alienated his subordinates and peers, and before his second anniversary was ignominiously fired. As a result of the organization's impatience, it lost market share and several key people while sales slid and margins eroded. After this fiasco, it called Heidrick & Struggles back to repair the damage. Following a thorough search, a candidate was selected who should have been in the role from the beginning.

According to Boyd Williams, senior vice president of human resources at DHL Express Asia Pacific, the decision to hire internally or externally depends on the situation. "If I were looking for significant organization transformation, then I'd be more inclined to go external," he says. "If I'm not, then I'm probably more inclined to look internally—but this is an oversimplified way of looking at things."

Hiring externally has a number of challenges. The more seniority a position carries, the greater the chance for failure. Unlike middle managers, new senior executives are immediately in the spotlight. At many companies in Asia, a new executive will be confronted with a sink-or-swim situation—either adapt to the new culture or drown, leaving the company with little more than an expensive lesson. An internal hire, on the other hand, has proven ability to operate within the company's culture.

So why not, then, stick with internal candidates? While certainly safer in the short term, relying only on internal promotions can lead to far greater long-term problems for an organization. A good case in point is the global pharmaceutical sector. Traditionally, this was an industry where companies tended to hire from within, and when they did hire externally, it was usually from another pharmaceutical firm.

Although this served the sector well for decades, the pharmaceutical industry has grown progressively more challenging, with additional competitors, fewer blockbuster drugs, and narrower margins. As a result, pharmaceutical firms have explored ways in which they can become more efficient, while hiring first-class talent. The best marketing people, however, come from companies with very low margins and a high consumer orientation like Procter & Gamble, Unilever, and Kraft. The best finance directors come from high-volume/low-cost manufacturing industries like semiconductors, and the top supply chain group comes from the automobile industry. It is to these sectors that pharmaceutical companies have turned in a bid to upgrade their human capital.

"If we are hiring somebody for a core industry discipline, then we usually hire within the sector," says Soma Mohanty Garg, director of human resources, Asia at Jones Lang LaSalle. "There are, however, situations where leadership in core disciplines can be extremely effective in turning an organization or discipline around, so while core technical functions probably need to come from within the industry, leadership talent can come from outside the sector."

Executives from other companies and other sectors bring in fresh ideas and processes, particularly in key functional areas such as human resources, finance, and supply chain management. What's more, a senior hire in one discipline will bring a wealth of ideas and thoughts that can improve other parts of an organization.

Aside from the acquisition of best practices, looking outside for talent helps an organization benchmark itself against the best in class. Many top corporations put internal candidates through the same interview process for key roles that they use for external candidates. Often, they will work with impartial external consultants to objectively compare their people with those available externally.

Whether an external hire succeeds often depends on the company's strong, forward-looking human resources team, which understands a company's business strategy and puts systems in place to ensure new executives adjust to its culture. They provide the new executive with a mentoring and coaching network to serve as a guide through the critical first 12 months on the job. As for the individual executives, they should refrain from making radical changes as much as possible until they do understand the culture.

Pierre Cohade, president, Asia Pacific Region for Goodyear Tire & Rubber Company, says Goodyear has a rigorous on-boarding process that lasts three months for new senior-level hires. The process includes trips to production locations and different countries as well as formal mentoring and an external coaching program. After six months, a 360-degree appraisal is conducted with the new executive. Interestingly, Goodyear's on-boarding efforts apply not only to external candidates but also to internal executives taking on new roles.

Ultimately, the question to hire from within or outside an organization has no single correct answer, but clever companies answer yes to both. They promote from within when possible, provided their internal talent is first rate, and from outside when they realize their internal resources fail to stack up to external benchmarks. The company must also ensure that new senior executives have the support they need to adapt to their new culture, which will help align their abilities with the organization's strategic objectives.

The Candidate Is King

Attracting and developing talent in today's globalized world is often on the minds of business leaders. One recent candidate for a high-level position at a large local company, however, wonders if Singapore's managers are getting the message. When he arrived for his interview, he was kept waiting for 45 minutes, and when his interviewer arrived, he made no apology for the delay. The 30-minute interview that followed was a casual, offhand affair, and the candidate was notified by e-mail that he had not received the job. "I got the impression the interviewer had made up his mind before he even met me," said the candidate later.

While this is an extreme case, it highlights the attitudes of a surprising number of managers in the region. Simply put, the prevailing attitude is that companies choose their people. In today's competitive landscape, however, it is not companies choosing the best people but the best people choosing companies. The global war for talent is over, and talent has won: talent has plenty of opportunities to choose from throughout the region and around the world.

For companies seeking to develop strong leadership teams in this tight talent market, it is crucial that managers develop world-class recruiting processes benchmarked not just against other companies in the region but also against the best in class globally. They need to clearly define roles, both in terms of responsibilities and of the skills and personality traits required for success. When the interviews begin, managers must work hard to maintain objectivity. They must treat every candidate with the utmost respect. Today's unsuccessful candidates could well be perfect for some future job openings—but they will remember a past snub, and probably tell their friends about it.

Once new employees are aboard, a formal induction process should be in place to greet them. As a rule of thumb, the more senior a hire is, the more comprehensive the induction process needs to be. New hires often fail to appreciate how different a new corporate culture is from what they have known in the past. To address this, companies should utilize coaching and mentoring programs that help new hires deal with the nuances of a new corporate culture. Such programs can substantially shorten the time it takes for a new hire to become a productive member of the team. Unfortunately, few companies have conversations with internal candidates who were passed over for the role when a new executive starts. To maintain morale, it is best to have clear discussions with these people, explaining the reasons for the decision to pass them over. Opportunities for career development for the internal candidate should be clearly addressed, which also lays the foundation for a good relationship between the external hire and the internal candidate.

Retention is of vital importance. Every employee eventually leaves, but extending the time an employee stays maximizes benefits to the company. Aside from competitive compensation and perks, one powerful retention strategy is to outline clear career paths for employees, particularly those who have been identified as high potentials. Another well-tested retention strategy for future leaders is that of job rotation. Multinationals are particularly strong at this, owing to their vast geographic reach. They often send high potentials for extended job assignments overseas, thereby developing dynamic leaders with a global perspective. While Singapore's companies may lack the sheer reach of multinational corporations, many with regional operations offer exciting growth opportunities for ambitious future leaders. Rotations are most successful if a company can provide an executive with a clear reentry strategy in the home market.

To successfully compete in today's hiring environment where the candidate is king, companies need an arsenal of world-class practices and processes that can bring in the right people and then develop their careers. Unfortunately, while many companies lay claim to the title "employer of choice," many fail to realize what this term implies: that the choice lies not with the company, but with the candidate.

Interim Options

When Nine Network CEO David Gyngell resigned without notice, saying his position had become untenable due to "increasingly unhelpful and multi-layered management systems," he pitched the company owned by the Packers, Australia's richest family, into a crisis.

Former CEO Sam Chisholm was quickly installed as interim boss. But it took eight months to find a replacement for Gyngell. The period of uncertainty ended when the popular entertainer Eddie McGuire was named. The damage to companies when a key executive leaves suddenly for any reason, be it disagreement with a new direction, illness, or even death, can be considerable. Competitors can surge ahead, promising new opportunities to senior staff, who may be overburdened or destabilized and thus likely to choose to leave. And the cost to replace senior executives can range between two and three times each individual's salary.

Apart from situational departures, the crisis at the top of corporate Australia is exacerbated by the rolling retirement of Baby Boomers (those born between 1946 and 1964), who began stepping down in 2002. Many of them will retire in 2008, and by 2011 the oldest boomers will reach 65.

Additional strain is being caused by what mentoring executive Bill Brown calls "the age of enlightenment" or leaving management ranks light on bench strength during downsizings that started in the late 1990s and continue through restructuring after restructuring.

While Chisholm was an experienced hand at Nine Network and well-known to the Packer family, it is rare to find such an interim executive just waiting in the wings. Brown says companies also are reluctant to appoint interim executives for fear that they will not bring the high level of commitment required if the role is just temporary.

Brown is passionate about the value interims bring to a company facing short-term problems, such as a business crisis or sudden demotion or retrenchment. His enthusiasm is not surprising. He has seen the world of interims from both sides of the fence. He admits that as a senior manager, he resisted hiring them, but once he became an interim himself, was astounded at the value of such an appointment.

"You are totally focused on a particular task, without needing to be drawn into the day-to-day issues of the company, and can devote your full 10 to 12 hours a day on that task," Brown says. "You deliver results quickly, and because you're an interim, you're not threatening any of the senior management team."

When Brown went to Cement Australia for a four-month role tackling an IT issue, he was commended by a senior executive for taking on a near-impossible task. "I didn't have to worry about the factories producing, the trains arriving on time, or whether the company had enough cement," he says. "I just did the job."

An often-overlooked quality that former senior executives bring to interim roles is political savvy, Brown continues. "You need someone politically astute enough to know what will and won't work."

Success Through Failure

University of Sydney COO and deputy vice chancellor Bob Kotic, former CFO of the financial services company ING, says he started to employ interims in the late 1990s because he was looking for mature business managers able to tackle a range of issues that could only be solved by someone who had been exposed to different industries and situations.

"I didn't just want people who would jump up and down in the same spot," Kotic says. "I wanted someone who was able to assess all of the contingencies and then find the best solution—you need to be able to know when the organization is going north or south."

Kotic says he found that executives with "a few failures under their belt" were particularly useful, and believes that interims are low risk. "If you've got the wrong person, you part company quickly," he said. He has also converted two interims to full-time staff. Kotic likes interims because they "don't over-think" problems, which 70 percent of the time are related to profitability, finances, and expenses.

Another fan of interims is Cement Australia's former human resources general manager Wayne Beel. He says chief executives and senior managers often do not fully understand the value of interims. "It's expensive not to employ them," he says. "If companies delay replacing a key executive, those left are distracted, their workload is doubled, targets are not achieved, and the leadership loses the confidence of the senior management because they're not achieving the targets."

Interims need a champion at the CEO or senior HR level, says Beel. If there's not high-level buy-in, divisional heads are "waiting around for recruitment permission." It took nine months to find one key executive at Cement Australia, he adds.

"You can get an interim in a fortnight, when it would take four to six to nine months to get a \$200,000-plus executive," and even then, the danger of one candidate falling over is high.

While such talent doesn't seem to be cheap at around US\$2,000 a day, an experienced C-level executive used to delivering results efficiently in fact works out to be much less expensive than management consultants (at up to US\$3,500 a day). Not only that, but consultants usually depart leaving a single document that still has to be implemented. Interims also do not demand sign-on or exit fees, and if they don't work out, they can be quickly replaced.

Another benefit for the corporation is that interim executives may turn out to be so desirable that they are asked to stay on board. But not all want a permanent role, preferring the variety of tasks and flexibility of lifestyle offered by their new career.

Interim executives fall into three main categories:

- Interim executives brought in for a fixed term
- Interim-to-permanent executives
- Project executives brought in for pre- to post-implementation

Apart from the cost, a major benefit of interim executives is experience. They have been in the situation before, and can mentor staff under them. The benefits of their experience can't be measured in purely monetary terms, as they often have an effect within the culture long after they have left. The adage that you cannot beat experience rings true.

As companies constantly reorganize to meet competitive challenges and executives themselves develop a "free-agent" mentality as a result of diminishing loyalty, the gaps at executive levels are becoming increasingly obvious.

The use of interims is growing rapidly in Australia and is already widespread in Britain, with an estimated 20 percent of appointments being interims. According to a much-quoted survey, project leaders are by far the most common interims, with around 50 percent of all interims being in this category. Interim finance executives are the second most popular category, with human resources leaders coming in third.

The departure of a top executive often leads companies to survey possible internal candidates and, if they do not find anyone suitable, they go out into the wider market. Often, a manager further down the tree may be a year or two away from being able to take the top job, and an interim executive can act as a mentor and coach.

Former National Australia Bank human resources executive Bessie Vaneris filled an interim HR role in Melbourne with the Boston-based smartcard operator Keane Inc. While there, she helped introduce a public transit ticketing system for the state of Victoria. Former executives hoping to "step lightly into retirement" shouldn't consider interim roles, she says. "Flexibility in the interim job description means working five or six days a week—not the three- or four-day week that some may be hoping for," she says. "But we can take time off between assignments. You can get a decent break of a month or so."

Vaneris says the interim executive should be prepared to stay longer than the initial brief might indicate. "My initial five-week role was extended to more than 10 months." The advantage of interims, says Vaneris, is that companies get "exactly what they want" in work that is often project-driven.

She got into interim work following a long career in financial services, where she honed her business skills—and flexibility—through multiple corporate reorganizations.

When asked what policy companies should adopt for interims, her philosophy is to have a flexible workforce aligning stakeholder needs and to have a blend of the following factors:

- Permanent employees with access to full-time, part-time and flexible work practices, such as some days working from home
- Contractors hired for specific assignments
- Short-term interim professionals, as well as more generic skills

Lifestyle Benefits

Former BHP Billiton human resources executive Ross James also enjoys the ability to take extended periods of time off between assignments. If he had not been an interim, he says, he would not have been able to act as a volunteer at the 2006 Commonwealth Games in Melbourne.

The 54-year-old, who took an interim HR role with the Carter Holt Harvey timber division, Radius, plans to visit Vietnam and travel around Ireland between roles, and may try the interim-to-permanent path if he finds the right opportunity.

With two of his four children still in college, he is looking to "create a mix of opportunities" over the next five to 10 years. He says the advantage of interims is that they are able to "go in, manage the tough calls, and do what has to be done" without being restrained by competition at the executive level or day-to-day issues.

Experienced former executives with cross-industry experience can also identify a problem that may elude more industry-based executives. When the Australian Red Cross Blood Service hired former Cochlear and IBM Consulting executive Vic Morrant, they thought they had a marketing crisis on their hands. The head of marketing had left along with several senior executives, and stocks of blood had fallen despite the significant amounts of money being spent on television advertising.

The solution turned out to be not to hammer the marketing budget harder, but rather to restore the confidence of the state-based divisions in the organization's central marketing management, and use inside experience to plan how best to address the blood stocks issue. Once core relationship issues were exposed and addressed, the state-based divisions united to apply a quick fix, and blood stocks rose to record levels. "Irrespective of how you define a problem, the key to it is always that someone in the organization did not do what was needed to be done," Kotic says.

The use of interims will only expand as gaps continue to appear in the fabric of today's fast-changing corporate world. Interims won't just be professionals parachuted into tough spots to fix urgent problems; they will evolve to become a permanent part of an increasingly flexible management structure.

5
EXECUTIVE TALENT MANAGEMENT

Multinational companies often struggle to manage their Asian leadership teams, but a more proactive approach by both sides can prevent unnecessary leadership turnover.

Long-Distance Relationships and How to Manage Them

Many corporate leaders in the West and regional managers in Asia can relate to troubled long-distance relationships. A few years ago, one major US corporation sent an executive with no experience in Asia to be president of its Asia Pacific operations. He spent a year getting used to his new environment and 18 months changing things for the corporate headquarters, and then returned to the United States. The company hired a new president from the region, but he lasted only two years. He lacked the trust and confidence of the head office, which balked at the changes he proposed. It subsequently replaced him with another executive from the corporate office—in five years, the company had three different presidents for the region.

This kind of leadership turnover is bad for staff morale and detrimental for relationships with joint venture partners and distributors. What's more, it makes stakeholders question a company's commitment to Asia, and that ultimately hurts profits. The foreign companies most successful in Asia are the ones that have had stable leadership teams throughout the years and strong succession planning programs for the region. Another characteristic of such organizations is a thorough understanding of Asia's unique challenges and issues back at the head office, along with many top managers boasting successful work experience in Asia.

Leaders sent to Asia from the corporate headquarters have strong ties to their colleagues at home, who know them and trust their judgment. However, they lack regional knowledge. Instead, they probably have a network of friends and allies in the company, which helps them to gauge the political winds back home and subtle changes in company strategy and direction. Leaders hired in the region have no such ties, but their market knowledge and cultural awareness will be greatly superior, and they won't need to go through the trauma of moving. Unfortunately, the lack of connection with the head office puts such executives at a great disadvantage and often results in their failure.

Gone Native

Leaders who come out from the corporate headquarters can also suffer from this connection gap. As executives settle into their regional role, the head office may start seeming very far away. The requests for information and updates can become irritating, particularly if the regional manager sees the requests as adding no value to day-to-day business. When this happens, regional managers are prone to falling out of touch with the political landscape at the head office and may fail to read the signs about what the corporate headquarters is thinking.

It is therefore crucial that senior managers sitting in the United States or Europe establish a clear communications strategy with their leaders in Asia. Conference calls should be scheduled as a regular, ongoing occurrence at times mutually convenient to both parties. For companies hiring a leader in Asia, it is important to have a comprehensive on-boarding strategy in place, which should involve the new executive from Asia spending time in the head office, becoming familiar with the company, and forming relationships with new colleagues.

If possible, the new executive's first assignments should include some project work at the head office: this will make it possible to meet people, establish a reputation, and become better acquainted with how the company is run. Once new executives return to Asia, corporate headquarters should find reasons for them to return every four to six weeks, if possible, for such events as planning sessions, the annual general meeting, training programs, and budget meetings.

For their part, executives in Asia need to be proactive about keeping in touch with the corporate office and work hard to manage expectations. One regional CEO of a software company recently learned this lesson the hard way. After having a good relationship with executives in the corporate headquarters for several years, he allowed his level of communication with them to decline. Then, after he missed just two quarters, the head office let him go, citing his failure to communicate as a major issue.

In the Trenches

For their part, leaders from Europe and the United States could do a better job of familiarizing themselves with Asia. Although the region constitutes only a small portion of sales for most multinational companies, their future growth lies in the vast, growing middle classes of China and India. Big markets such as Indonesia, Vietnam, Thailand, Korea and even the Philippines also offer substantial growth and opportunity.

The only way to really understand Asia and its bewildering array of cultures and economies is to visit in person—and not merely to sit in air-conditioned boardrooms in comfortable, Westernized cities such as Singapore and Hong Kong. Trips should include visits to the frontier regions, as it were, where future growth resides. Such visits will give executives insights into the opportunities and challenges in Asia, and provide a superb chance to connect with the region's second and third tiers of leadership.

As Asia develops, it will become an increasingly competitive region in which to succeed. To enjoy this success, the right regional leadership is crucial, but both corporate and regional leaders must remain constantly aware of the dangers inherent in long-distance relationships. Both parties must strive to keep the lines of communication open. Regional leaders should be forthcoming about their business and strive to understand the head office's viewpoint, while those in the head office should make a real effort to better understand the dynamism and diversity of Asia.

New Challenges in a Virtual World

Executives are grappling with new ways of managing their staff as the world grows flatter and leadership teams are decentralized and virtualized. The old face-oriented offices have given way to virtual communities of outsource partners, offshore teams, and globally distributed workforces.

On any given day, 42 percent of IBM's workforce of 330,000 workers do not report to the location where they are based. The company's human resources head, Randy MacDonald, says the past 10 years can be characterized as the fall of the traditional business empire and the rise or emergence of global collaborative and virtual empires.

This new paradigm is enabled by the proliferation of communications technologies, broadband and changing business models. In a faster-paced, more competitive world, executives must be more flexible and agile, and must acquire new communication and management skills.

Paradoxically, a virtual world calls for greater relationship-building efforts than in traditional teams or organizations. MacDonald says that many millions of dollars have been spent on teaching employees verbal communication skills. "In this new world of virtualization and visualization, we haven't taught these skills. Going back to some of the basics in this evolving world of work will be critical."

Eric Lesser, head of human capital research for IBM's consulting practice, agrees. "With a virtual world, you change the dynamic around social capital and you change the value of the relationships that you have. On the one hand, you get to expand greatly the number of relationships—but they also become more difficult to maintain in terms of geography, time zone and culture."

Lesser adds, "What this means is that relationship maintenance becomes increasingly more important. You need to pay more attention to relationships."

He describes three keys to communication for executives in the new, disembodied organizations:

- Connections
- Relationships
- Common context

"It's more important to maintain your network and your connections by having regular face-to-face meetings, and then to build a relationship of trust, and to understand the context in which you find your distributed workers," says Lesser.

While flexibility is valued and technology enables flexibility, he adds that executives must take care to maintain balance. Without balance, an executive can quickly be overwhelmed. Boundaries should be set and respected. "I can do an event with my kid from four to six o'clock but will be happy to get back online at night—that's not a stigma within groups I work with at IBM," Lesser says.

"The challenge, though, is your ability to shut it off. Executives and managers need to help workers to define rules about when they're available and when they're not—to help them draw boundaries and guidelines," he says.

Lesser says that one of the biggest challenges is making the right connections between people globally—"How do I find the person who can answer my question with one phone call or maybe two rather than five or six?"

According to Lesser, businesses need an organizing framework or taxonomy for their staff software so staff can rapidly find key people. Once the experts are located, enabling technologies such as instant messaging, conference calls, and videoconferencing take over.

"But technology by itself is not enough. If you have key sites or project teams located away from the main office, you have to give people the opportunity to meet face-to-face at least once. You need to build up trust which comes only from a deep understanding of what people do, their values and motivations."

Truth Through Trust

Mark Allaby, former Toronto-based financial services partner for Accenture, says that the first rule for virtual workforces is that relationships need to be established ahead of the virtualization.

He says Accenture runs many management meetings by conference calls and also uses multiple virtual channels such as instant messaging and videoconferencing. "It works well in a workforce where people know each other, where there's a relaxed environment and trust, so that participants are comfortable saying what they think and asking direct questions."

But Allaby says that with large offshore project teams, the challenge is greater.

"When running large project teams in India and Manila, we didn't just pick up the phone and say, 'Right, guys, we're a team, let's get to it.' We had to go and build relationships. We sent people at all levels from the onshore teams and had some of the offshore guys come onshore. If you don't do this, you just get a lot of talking but no real communication."

According to Allaby, e-mail is the biggest killer man has ever invented. "People start flinging e-mails back and forth and never resolve anything. You need to force yourself onto the phone, talk things through and listen to other people's point of view. Some of the disciplines around good meeting habits need to be relearned in the virtual environment. You need to really try to understand what they're getting at, as opposed to just pushing your own topic."

Executives need to be both more flexible and more aware of staff slipping into technology and out of communication.

Interpersonal skills such as team building, collaboration, and relationship focus are critical to powerful and effective leadership in a virtual world. Leaders need to propel their teams into face-to-face relationships and avoid the situation that one executive described to us, where a group of people—occupying three different floors of the same building—regularly communicated via teleconference!

Winning Trust, Driving Success

To succeed, a leader's precise role and responsibilities must be clear to the team and to management—and to the leader, too.

Leadership roles in large organizations are no longer clear-cut. The matrix organization structures common in Western corporations and increasingly popular with Asian companies create great flexibility for a company.

Unfortunately, this web of "dotted reporting lines" means a new leader's role, in relation to the team of direct reports, falls into several shades of gray—and one major criticism of matrix structures is the culture of unaccountability they can engender. To ensure success, it is imperative that leaders have a good idea what their role and responsibility is vis-à-vis various team members—many of whom could be in different countries and time zones.

"I believe leadership is a privilege bestowed on you, and it can be taken away very quickly," says Kenneth Lewis, chairman, president, and CEO of Bank of America. "You can manage someone or a group of people, but you can't get to a real level of performance through leadership if it's not bestowed on you by the people who believe in you. The critical link here is trust: if you don't establish that bond of trust and you're not always credible, then you will eventually lose the ability to lead."

To win this trust, leaders must secure a clear mandate from their own management.

A cornerstone of effective leadership is discussing performance with team members and reviewing projects on a regular basis, ensuring that people deliver on their commitments: even the best plans will fail if execution is lacking.

While leaders must play a major role in both planning and execution, they must not take it as a given that individual team members will automatically appreciate their input.

A sales manager, for example, may feel it is entirely proper to visit clients, but it is essential that the sales team view their manager's role in the same way. An important first step for all leaders is to determine if upper management agrees that their job scope comprises certain activities, and then this vision must be conveyed to their teams clearly and unequivocally.

It is also important that team leaders make sure their compensation is tied to the success of their team members. This is particularly important at professional services companies, where a manager may still have direct responsibility for generating business. To be successful, leaders must know that when appraisal time comes, their own success will be tied to the performance of their various group members.

Pat Mitchell, a former president and CEO of the US Public Broadcasting System, is a firm believer in rewarding leaders for team performance: "Our bonus plans are based on evaluating. For example, if you're head of promotion and we have very few promotion dollars, have you targeted those dollars toward programming so that it has significantly impacted this market or that market? We have a point system that is based on how well you manage your resources, your budget, and your people."

Another element to establishing a mandate is winning over the informal opinion leaders in your team. Staff members who have been in a team for a long while will have endless opinions about their role and the general company. To a greater or lesser degree they will have an impact on the morale and viewpoint of other team members. A new manager would do well to identify such individuals early on, and find ways to get them involved in key processes. If handled correctly they can offer valuable feedback about the wider group and make suggestions that benefit the business.

Leaders should also keep time free to attend group meetings, perhaps as an "outside observer." Attending such meetings demonstrates interest in what the groups are doing, as well as enthusiasm for group activities. What's more, leaders can gain valuable insights into the nature of the opportunities and challenges their people face on a regular basis. Subtly following up on action items discussed in meetings will help ensure key projects and initiatives are moving forward.

In short, success depends on making connections with people—and then working to keep them alive. "The secret is to build an emotional network between people," says Dana Ardi, human capital partner of JP Morgan Partners. "It's about making connections and building a community. It doesn't happen overnight. A lot of organizations don't value connectivity as much as they should, so they may not create opportunities to build an emotional network. You really have to bring people together on a variety of levels and allow for genuine dialogue and interaction to make the whole team effective."

Important points toward building trust:

- Obtain a detailed understanding of your role's scope from senior management.
- Show an interest in team activities such as meetings, and follow up on team action plans.
- Win over key influencers in the team.
- If possible, have your remuneration tied to the performance of the team.

Dealing with Prima Donnas

Top-performing prima donnas have been the bane of many a leader. A deft touch is essential to handling them well and keeping the team happy.

These people before have vexed all experienced leaders: difficult, challenging employees who also happen to be brilliant at their jobs, and who are well aware of their value. In other words, prima donnas. Their work is flawless, perhaps inspired, and they carry a disproportionate amount of the team's load. The vast majority of leaders bend over backward to appease such people, but others on the team could well detect double standards, causing a serious morale issue. What's more, promoting a prima donna to a leadership position is likely to create more problems.

"Top grading is absolutely important, but keep in mind that there are lots of people in the top 20 percent who should never be put in a leadership position," says Frederick W. Smith, founder, chairman, and CEO of FedEx Corporation. "The key is for the organization and the individual both to understand and be satisfied with that position.... Many organizations get into trouble in this regard, because the only avenue they have for financially rewarding top performers is to move them into management positions."

Often, prima donnas' aggressive behavior helps feed the high self-esteem that gives them the confidence to outperform and punch above their weight, but other team members can see their behavior as arrogant. An objective of leaders should therefore be to change this behavior and then wean prima donnas off this source of self-esteem, whether through direct praise and recognition or by satisfying other needs. A careful approach is essential in order to keep the morale of both the prima donna and the team intact.

However attractive procrastination may be, it is essential for leaders to address prima donna behavior as soon as it rears its head. The sooner a leader acts, the better the chances of success. When confronting prima donnas, describe the behavior that needs to change. Be specific, and have concrete examples ready: the individual must see that the feedback has its basis in fact.

Having laid out the problem as candidly as possible, explain why the issue is of concern, taking care to focus on specific behaviors, not the prima donna's personality in general. Having done so, try to find out the underlying reasons for the individual's behavior. Is it an issue of personality? Problems outside the office? In these discussions, it may be a good idea to include a third party, preferably somebody the prima donna trusts and respects.

Be sure to convey that you are not merely forcing the individual to heed your will, you are trying to improve the overall performance and morale of the team. Focusing on how change can help the individual's career development is also useful, as people want to know what their payoff will be for changed behavior.

If an individual, for instance, consistently rubs key people the wrong way, point out that alienating such people could hurt the individual's success in the future.

"Leadership communication, to actually move people to act, must be both authentic and frequent," says David S. Pottruck, former president and co-CEO of Charles Schwab. "It is a rare combination of listening and speaking that lets others know you care, and inspires them with possibilities that they may not, without you, be able to see."

Finally, get the individual's ideas for solving the problem, and a commitment to doing so. Be sure to offer your support and make available the resources that may be needed to effect change, such as external professional help or communications skills training. Finally, work with the prima donna to develop an action plan, setting a specific date for follow-up.

The final (and arguably the most important) element in dealing with prima donnas is the issue of special treatment. Consider this: in many corporations, who is likely to receive a harsher performance review, the team player who is a mediocre performer, or the prima donna who is a star performer? While the temptation to indulge in favoritism is one to which many managers succumb, ultimately such a course is shortsighted and detrimental to long-term goals, particularly given the ever-increasing emphasis on teamwork in today's world.

The best game plan for dealing with prima donnas:

- Remember that aggressive behavior can be a source of self-esteem for prima donnas; leaders need to find other ways to fuel this self-esteem.
- Act as soon as prima donna behavior becomes apparent—avoid procrastination.
- When speaking with a prima donna, offer specific examples of the behavior that needs to change—avoid making it an issue of general personality.
- Stress how a change in behavior will help benefit the individual over the long run.
- Avoid favoritism: in today's team-centric world, favoritism can be dangerous for morale.

Fighting Office Warfare

Office conflicts are bad news for corporate performance, but by acting quickly and mediating, leaders can settle things peacefully and get people back on track.

It can start quietly: a negative remark in a meeting, an e-mail that comes across the wrong way, or a procedural change that somebody is not notified about. However they start—and the list of possibilities is endless—office conflicts among team members can (at best) create a hostile, negative work environment, or (at worst) hurt business performance, resulting in a loss of focus and missed goals.

Effective leaders are adept at spotting conflicts before they become unmanageable, resolving them in a way that saves face for the feuding parties and renews the team's focus on long-term objectives.

"The skill of CEOs and senior managers to create a vision that everyone in the company can identify with, and be motivated and excited by, is critically important," says Mohanbir Sawhney, a leading professor at Northwestern University's Kellogg School of Management. "Leaders are evangelists more than anything else, and need to constantly align people's and the business's activities toward the larger goal. Infusing the organization with a sense of purpose and a mission that is larger than profits is very important, because it will motivate people, and that, in turn, will determine your ability to retain good people; thus, ultimately, it will determine your organization's success in the marketplace."

Office conflicts have the potential to sabotage the long-term goals Sawhney speaks of. Such conflicts have several telltale signs. Conflict can take the form of persistent squabbling between two team members, perhaps even extending to blatant put-downs, remarks aimed not at resolving issues but at diminishing a rival's self-esteem and confidence. It can take the form of regularly criticizing another team member, openly or covertly, to other colleagues.

Office conflict can be conducted underground, with two team members ignoring each other and limiting interaction to the bare minimum. Regardless of the nature the conflict takes, the leader's role is to play both mediator and evangelist, helping people move beyond squabbles and refocus on business objectives.

Leaders really have no choice but to get involved; interpersonal conflicts are difficult for people to resolve themselves. It is human nature to avoid addressing issues—letting problems simmer beneath the surface, poisoning the attitudes of the people involved, and eventually spreading to more team members. Office conflicts tend to arise in a few key areas: over facts (a basic misunderstanding that can be easily resolved), over process and methods (people agree on objectives, but not how they should be attained), over purpose (people have different goals), and over ideals (people have different beliefs and principles). Of these four, differences over ideals are the most difficult to resolve.

To step in effectively, you need to take a consultative approach, listening to the issue from both perspectives and identifying common ground between both viewpoints. It is important to frame the discussion not in terms of various points of difference but in terms of the long-term objectives of the team, where success is an equally desirable outcome for all team members.

In a conflict resolution meeting, sit down with both parties and describe the counterproductive behavior that has been observed, stressing how this behavior will impact the team's performance. Then get each person to describe their grievance in detail. Following this, have both employees describe the other's point of view, and then identify specific points of agreement and disagreement. Having listened to all this, you can ask the two team members for ideas on how to proceed.

This process will help both employees see the common ground they share—often, they will be surprised to learn how much they have in common. It will also help them take ownership of the problem and see the long-term benefits for resolving the issue. At that point, you can help outline the steps both parties need to take, with success more likely if both parties make small concessions from the very outset, thus saving face for both. For all this to succeed, however, it is imperative to spot the problem early and act decisively to resolve it.

Key tips for resolving office conflicts:

- Act quickly when the signs of a conflict emerge.
- Sit down with the warring parties and outline why it is in their long-term interest to resolve their differences.
- Listen as they outline their grievances.
- Have each party summarize the other's point of view, encouraging them to note points of common ground.
- Encourage both sides to make some face-saving concessions, and get agreement on the steps both parties need to take to resolve the conflict.

Managing a Multi-Generational Workforce

Businesses competing for the same talent are starting to appreciate that their methods of hiring, motivating, and retaining talent need to be reviewed. For the first time in history, we have four distinct generations in the workforce:

- *The Traditionalists*: Employed for between 30 and 40 years, with a basket of skills and knowledge that may not be recognized, appreciated, or understood by the younger executives managing them.
- *The Baby Boomers*: Often used to a more hierarchical style of management. As executives, they tend to adopt a command-and-control style unless coached otherwise.
- *Generation X*: Intensely self-focused post-Boomers, born during the 1960s and 1970s, who often lack loyalty to an employer. Without clear career goals, Gen-Xers may place family and community above work requirements.

- *Generation Y*: Currently graduating from university, Gen-Yers value partnering and collaboration but seem to be uncomfortable in hierarchies and rigid structures. They rarely seek responsibility, and if given it, they seek to share.

It takes perceptive leaders to juggle the competing demands of this diverse workforce while keeping them motivated and focused. Different roles call for different skills and age levels. More experienced older workers may suddenly demand more money while younger groups seek greater flexibility and creative reward options, such as additional vacation or sabbaticals.

Similarly, while older employees are interested in retirement security as well as salaries and bonuses, share plans, investment plans, and medical coverage, they may also seek flexible hours. In Australia, for example, the Fairfax newspaper group brought in a "sea change" program for senior writers and editors, which allowed them to scale back their working days and start to move toward part-time work.

Younger workers are more interested in career development and the chance to gain more educational qualifications. They also want better child care. They are after work-life balance and don't want to repeat what they see as the mistakes of their workaholic parents.

The Lost Generation

Paolo Emilio Testa, former EDS Asia Pacific HR director, believes the task facing employers managing multiple generations is challenging, with no easy answers. But he suggests that accurate performance measurement is the key, as it provides a metric on which all can agree.

"Cultural transformation is also crucial," Testa says. "One of the biggest issues is how to win back our older people—we have to bring them back to the company. They are disillusioned, tired, and cynical. That's a bigger challenge, as opposed to rewarding them. They are in many ways the lost generation."

US-based researchers Tamara Erickson and Bob Morison of the Concours Group agree. They say older workers have traditionally placed great value on financial security and are uncomfortable with the ambiguity common in contemporary business.

In their book *Workforce Crisis* (coauthored with Ken Dychtwald and published by the Harvard Business School Press), they advise businesses to think of retirement as an opportunity to keep talent around, rather than as a way to phase people out. They refer to chemical company Monsanto, which helps retirees who leave the company in good standing to return in part-time roles.

Testa says the middle section of the workforce, mainly Boomers, needs to be given fresh assignments to prevent stagnation. "But the younger workers want to know immediately when they are hired, 'What's next?' They want to know about their career. They are keen to understand the company's expectations and what they can give the company."

He says younger workers don't want to stay in one role too long, either. "They want opportunities across the board as well as to progress in the organizational structure—to grow their experience company-wide." It is perhaps by having seen specialists made redundant that they realize the importance of broader skills and learning. Flexibility and maximizing career options almost appear to be ends in themselves.

Demographer Bernard Salt of KPMG says the retrenchment of loyal executives at the peak of the last recession changed the attitudes of Generations X and Y toward corporations. "The Ys learned the lesson that they should be loyal to none but their own interests. As they entered the workforce soon after the turn of the century, they remained loyal to the corporation only for as long as their job contributed to their commercial capital."

Salt says the emotional needs of Generation Y were fostered and supported by coddling Boomer parents, as well as by a defined group of friends—now their work colleagues.

"The workplace of the Ys has become a platform for other and later strategic engagements. Their 'single-child' syndrome gives them the confidence to challenge the authority of Boomer management. Boomers at the same age were deferential," Salt says.

Global Roaming

Salt says Generation Y may be the first generation in many Asia Pacific nations to see their future offshore. "It has never occurred to many centers that they might need to develop defensive migration strategies to retain their best and brightest young citizens. They have always assumed that their migration problems relate to holding people at bay, not to holding on to their residents."

He says it's difficult enough now to retain the best Generation Y people, but what will it be like in a decade when representatives of Northern Hemisphere economies come on recruiting drives to cherry-pick our best graduates?

"Generation Y is not committed to the anchors that held young Boomers in their country: partner, children, mortgage. The international market for labor has freed up in the last decade. Skilled workers and populations are moving more freely into and out of Eastern Europe since the collapse of the Soviet Union and its member states. Hong Kong, China, and India have all moved into new economic and political paradigms.

"The centers of world trade, power, and influence that interface with this changing world are proving irresistible to bright, young, entrepreneurial—and unconnected—Ys from satellite nations such as Australia and New Zealand. For example, around one million Australians now live offshore; that's five percent of the Australian race floating around the globe in pursuit of work or a lifestyle."

HR Vice President Mark Ketzel of Yahoo Asia Pacific says age is not an issue facing his company. "We are only interested in people who can drive results."

"In the Internet sector, business and competition changes so quickly that a lot of people either select themselves in or out of this environment. If a certain generation doesn't feel they can optimize their success, or have their biggest contribution in a company where the competition shifts and it's very fast-paced, they self-select out."

Hong Kong-based Ketzel says Yahoo is honest and open with recruits about the types of skills it takes to succeed at the company. "We are looking for individuals who are comfortable with a lack of strict processes, who are able to deal with ambiguity, and who are smart. They must also be able to pick up on new trends and have the ability to multi-task."

He says the key for Yahoo in attracting and retaining people of all ages and cultures is its open, inclusive culture. "We differentiate success as being able to deliver results. People of any age who prefer a more hierarchical approach would not be comfortable and successful in this type of environment."

There are four things leaders can do to better manage multiple generations:

- Ensure open communication. Honestly address concerns. Being open and transparent will go a long way toward bringing issues into the open and retaining your best people.
- Respect the different values held by different age groups. This simply means being aware of the lack of loyalty of young people— and the possibly excessive loyalty of older people.

- Encourage intergenerational partnerships and collaboration. You need to teach the older workers to listen for the fresh ideas of the younger generation, and teach younger leaders to seek out and value the experience of the older people.
- Remain flexible. You have to be flexible for the fickle younger generation, but also look for ways to retain the knowledge—if not the days of work—of more experienced executives. They hold a lot of your corporate memory, which is better with you than with a competitor.

6

MENTORING, COACHING AND SETTING AN EXAMPLE

When sifting through candidates for top positions, one question Heidrick & Struggles often asks potential CEOs is: To what extent do you know you were doing other people's jobs for them? Many respond with something along these lines: "I've had to step in often—it's been a tough year and we needed to move fast to reach our targets. So I've stepped in and taken responsibility for projects to ensure they were done right."

On the surface, that sounds like a good answer—suggesting personal competence and willingness to jump into the breach when required. That may be fine for middle management, but it's deadly for C-level executives. The question then becomes; Why didn't you coach or mentor your employees to help them learn how to do it for themselves?

Make Yourself a Mentor, Coach

It's a skills failing for a CEO to rely on the maxim, "If you want it done right, do it yourself." That's unsustainable at the top levels of a company and creates staff dependency on the boss—not a good deployment of the talent you have at your disposal. It also suggests that the executive doesn't make time to share experience and help develop the staff—an "it takes too much time to help them, so I might as well do it myself" attitude. That may be good for followers, but it doesn't work for leaders. The old parable stands true today in creating a winning staff that works for you: Give people a fish, and they eat for a day. Teach them how to fish, and they eat for a lifetime.

Coaching and *mentoring* are often used interchangeably, but there are distinct differences between them:

MENTORS
- Share their own experience to help bridge the learning gap of the employee.
- Use interpersonal skills to connect their experience in a context that the employee understands and can apply to the current situation.
- Champion their charges—advocate for them within the company, pushing them into projects and assignments that help round out their skills.

COACHES
- Help employees help themselves—coaches don't teach from their experience, they help people make sense of their own experience.
- Use and help the employee develop intrapersonal skills—knowing yourself and asking yourself the right questions to make the right decisions.
- Employ a Socratic method, simply listening and asking the right questions.

For mentors, it's important that sharing experience doesn't become a form of prescription—"do what I did and you will succeed" is unlikely to be useful. While sharing of experience is important, it also carries the danger of putting blinders on the employee—times have changed and the situation is different. The lessons of the past must be applied to the new reality of the present and the challenges of the future.

For coaches, the key skill that needs to be developed is simple, yet often the most difficult for high fliers—listening and asking questions. It may seem in the moment better to spend five minutes telling an employee what to do than spend half an hour helping the employee figure it out. But in the long run, the latter method brings sustainable results instead of short-term fixes.

In Asia, those being mentored or coached often have a pervasive perception problem about what the activity means. Those who are being mentored often feel they've been anointed by upper management for big things. Those who are being coached feel that it's a remedial step, something that must be done to avoid bad reviews or even firing. Neither is true—both are necessary steps for any successful career, whether coaching and mentoring happens formally or—as is often the case—informally. Keep in mind that Tiger Woods has different coaches for different aspects of his game. No one would accuse Woods of being in need of remedial help in his career. He understands the importance of coaching.

The Gentle Art of Coaching

Coaching is an extremely powerful leadership tool, but there are several things a manager must remember before attempting to coach team members.

As CEO-turned-coach Jack Welch is widely reported to have said, the best executive is "an overburdened, overstretched executive, because he or she doesn't have the time to meddle, to deal in trivia or to bother people."

But one of the hardest things that newly minted executives find when they reach the top is the need to let go and focus on the strategic business drivers that will help carry the company forward. In fact, they have to forget about many of the technical aspects of their job that created their initial success.

Coaches can help unlock the inner strengths of leadership team members and encourage development of those strengths. Self-awareness varies among executives. While many are clear about their own weaknesses, most are only dimly aware of where their strengths lie.

It is often not until someone takes a close interest in helping these executives that their performance starts to improve. This is where coaching comes in. The first step for a leader who wishes to initiate coaching for a team is to earn their trust.

As mentioned earlier, a major part of leadership is unlocking team members' inner strengths and helping them develop these strengths. Self-awareness varies greatly at all levels, not just among managers. Even those who know their strengths may need time, effort, and patience to develop themselves, just as gifted athletes and artists require years of practice to perfect their skills. Often, performance will improve when somebody takes a close interest in helping people identify their true strengths and then perfect them.

"Trust is built through knowing that a leader cares about you," says Pottruck, "A leader simply has to be able to see and acknowledge other points of view, value them, and communicate appreciation for them.

The focus is not merely on answering questions, but rather on responding to people. The effective communicator knows the difference between 'Did he hear you?' and 'Do you feel heard?' One is a transaction, the other is a connection; and it is connection that inspires people to do their best work."

Coaching is far more than just managing. When dealing with direct reports, coaching means going beyond the day-to-day aspects of management and its tangible goals to help people build their strengths and develop skills and thought processes that will make them future leaders. A good manager can manage a team of followers effectively, but a good coach listens to people, identifying their needs and helping them grow. Management is about guiding; coaching is about inspiring.

Only by truly listening and fully understanding people can a leader become viewed as a coach who is committed to helping others achieve their goals. To ensure coaching happens, managers should set aside time in advance—for example, one hour every quarter—for coaching activities. For newer team members or those facing particularly challenging situations—for example, a new role, project, or team—coaching sessions can and should be scheduled more frequently.

Coaching, however, should not be limited to such sessions. Invariably, opportunities for coaching emerge in the daily rough-and-tumble of corporate life. Employees who are confused or frustrated, mired in indecision, or performing below standards could probably benefit from a coaching intervention. Regardless of whether the intervention is planned in advance or not, it's best to decide what key points you want to drive home, and to be aware of what motivates the individuals involved—money, recognition, or compliments. This knowledge makes it possible to frame the coaching discussion in a way that will appeal to the employee.

Another issue, particularly for managers in Southeast Asia, is the tyranny of distance. Often, managers find they are responsible for managing and coaching people overseas, operating in a completely different context, and with a completely different cultural background. Coaching from a distance is challenging, but there are ways to do it. Some managers ask colleagues in the employee's home country to help out with coaching. Managers who travel a great deal can set aside time during trips for coaching. It takes extra effort, but it can pay off handsomely.

When coaching an employee, a good first step is to ask how things are going, and then offer help. The language used is important here. Rather than telling someone you would like to see them, instead pose a question: "Are you free for a few minutes to discuss this? Maybe I can offer some help. Is now a good time or shall we grab some coffee later?"

In the coaching session itself, actively clarify the situation through questioning that will draw out specific facts—questions starting with words such as who, where, or what. Do not try to solve the problem, and avoid questions that may put people on the defensive. Such questions often start with words such as how or why, such as "Why did you fail to hit your sales numbers?" or "How could you allow this to happen?" If you hear yourself asking this kind of question, you need to take a step back. These words often signal an accusation.

"All the good-to-great leaders are superb at asking questions," says leadership expert and author Jim Collins. "Many have law degrees, and their legal backgrounds help appreciate a perspective of asking questions. Most people are uncomfortable about talking about themselves. Leaders need to listen carefully to the employee's answers and offer a viewpoint only where it may be helpful."[1]

Throughout the meeting, listen to the employee's answers and say only what the employee needs to move forward. If the problem is large and challenging, detailed feedback may be necessary. If a creative solution is called for, then perhaps offer suggestions that help an employee approach a problem from new directions. Toward the end of the discussion, agree on the next steps an employee needs to take, and get a commitment to action. Then offer your full support, and perhaps set a time for follow-up.

Done well, coaching offers a superb way to improve the performance of both individual employees and groups. For coaching to be successful, managers must first work to win the trust of their employees, time their coaching interventions carefully, ask the right questions, and most important, listen.

Tips on successful coaching:

- Remember that coaching is guiding, not telling or doing.
- Before a coaching session, whether planned or not, pause to decide on the key objectives you would like the session to achieve.
- Ask the right questions—and avoid questions that may put an employee on the defensive.
- Listen carefully to the answers to your questions, and offer your viewpoint only where it will be helpful to move the employee forward.

Dealing with an Underperformer

Good leaders are proactive at dealing with their underperformers. The business world is obsessed with nurturing its top performers. At good companies, such individuals are identified early and opportunities for them abound: overseas job postings, training, advanced degrees, and other programs to help their growth. Leading such individuals is relatively easy compared with managing underperformers, but improving the performance of laggards is one mark of the true leader.

"Ten percent of our population make up our group of superachievers, and we go to great lengths to retain and recognize them," says Eugene V. Polistuk, former CEO of supply chain firm Celestica. "The bottom 10 percent we work with to retrain and develop in an effort to enhance performance.... It is just as important to manage the bottom 10 percent as it is to manage the top performers."

Dealing with underperformers is challenging. Many managers find that efforts to deal with such individuals garner only mixed results, with the employee improving for a short while and then regressing. When this happens, managers become discouraged and give up trying to change things.

To achieve lasting results, managers need to be tenacious and make it clear they are serious. Most important, they must show they are eager to help as much as possible: employees are more likely to listen to a manager they feel is on their side.

Rarely do people underperform because they lack the competence for the job. Often, underperformance springs from low motivation, which could stem from an infinite range of problems. It is up to a leader to restore this motivation, helping an employee find a sense of meaning in the work at hand. The key is determining the root cause of the problem. Never rush to assumptions about why somebody is unproductive. A manager in the habit of having informal conversations with team members will find it easier to identify the root issue, be it something in the employee's personal life or problems at work.

The first step to resolving a performance issue is laying it on the table. Set a meeting in advance by describing the issue and asking the employee to give it some thought. Emphasize that you are looking for feedback and perspective. In the meeting itself, it is important to listen while making it clear that you have confidence in the employee. Finally, get agreement that the issue exists, discuss the causes, and review the individual's specific goals. Do not be surprised if the employee becomes defensive, but remember the problem is the issue at hand, not the employee per se. Listen carefully—by determining the root causes of the underperformance, you are on the way to resolution.

Try to discover things the employee feels stand in the way of improving, particularly things that feel uncontrollable, as a leader may be able to remove such obstacles. A leader should also offer ideas for improvement, and finally agree on specific actions both the leader and employee can take to bring the employee's performance to an acceptable level.

When broaching the issue of poor performance, it is important to be as diplomatic as possible, showing genuine empathy but making it clear it is up to them to improve things. Leaders often find this a difficult conversation to initiate, particularly given the countless other demands facing them. It is, however, essential to have this conversation as soon as possible, before a performance issue becomes a serious problem that drags down the entire team.

At the end of the meeting, set a follow-up date to review progress. After the meeting, send an e-mail detailing the action steps agreed upon. In follow-up meetings, be sure to acknowledge any progress made.

Of course, some employees simply will not improve. The reasons for this can vary, but carrying a weak performer for too long can be detrimental for team morale. Such situations have several solutions: avoid the issue and let higher management deal with it, or perhaps have the person transferred to another area, which in certain situations can help the employee improve. Failing these options, a leader can lobby to have the employee terminated.

"Leaders may not always be the most popular people in the organization, for they may be forced to make the tough decisions and point out what others may prefer to ignore," says Jeffrey Katz, former president and CEO of online travel company Orbitz. "But leaders know that applying their decisions in consistent and rational manner eventually creates consensus as others begin to share more fully in the vision and direction."

Steps for dealing with an underperformer:

- Be proactive: arrange a meeting to discuss the issue.
- Make sure the employee knows you are both on the same side.
- Agree on what the issue is—and the steps to change things.
- Write down the agreed action plan.
- Schedule subsequent meetings to review progress.

Dealing with underperformers is hard and may not make you popular, but the ability to do so is a hallmark of senior leadership.

Change the Culture and Improve Performance

Mentoring and coaching are essential steps for all top executives who want to be artful change agents for their companies. The most instructive lessons of change management come from the information technology aspect of any company, which can see seismic changes inside a business quarter.

Large corporations are now living or dying according to the speed with which they can change their information technology and systems. If they don't get their supply chain working right, and fast, you can bet that their closest competitor will soon be eating their lunch. Failing to take advantage of major technological advances or opportunities may result in being blindsided, forced out of business, or scrambling—expensively—to catch up.

But it's not just about the technology. The challenge today is to reengineer the entire culture of an organization so that its systems can be streamlined to enable it to compete effectively. As Peter Senge says in *The Fifth Discipline*, everyone in the company has to be on-board with the need for change and willing to participate in a new way of doing business. "People want change, they don't want to be changed," he says.

He gives three criteria for success: management commitment, universal approval, and appropriate measures and rewards. For "universal approval," read "culture change."

Successful change agents move quickly to outline the need for change, define the culture that will work best, and then set about getting the key teams on board. "On-boarding," as it is called, is critical to helping the new team and its members find traction and early momentum. Specific values and cultural norms need to be debated and defined, and set right at the outset to guide recruitment and team behaviors. Recruitment decisions must focus on the new culture fit, as well as on experience and competency.

Also critical is highly visible and wide-ranging executive change. In other words, changing the behaviors and values almost always requires rapidly changing the people. A new team is therefore needed. This usually comprises the best internal and external recruits. Coles Myer's Mahler says that of the 50 at the top of the IT tree when he took over in October 2002, only 11 are still in place today.

"I had to spill the top three layers," he recalls. "Everyone could reapply. Then we attacked the next layers down. We removed hundreds of people. Creating a new culture is more important than retaining the experience of the people in the company. The IT experience in telecommunications, retail, and banking is very similar. You don't need to be a retailer to do IT in retailing. But you do need people with the right behaviors and values."

Mahler needed to hit the ground running. Just months earlier, his CEO, John Fletcher, himself a newcomer (previously with Brambles), had announced high-risk plans for a logistics- and supply chain–led recovery operation for the retailer, whose processes were highly fragmented, to say the least.

"I'm a strong believer that you cannot achieve technological change unless you also bring about cultural change," Mahler says. "At Coles Myer, we have been able to achieve a breakthrough in leadership. I haven't had the time to do this in other companies."

Mahler, a Canadian, had a track record of success in turning around IT systems in customer-focused corporations, notably the Canadian media conglomerate Western International Communications and the major Belgian telecommunications company, Belgacom.

"At Coles Myer, we are successfully teaching people how to become leaders," Mahler says. "Managers can be the best technology people but have no experience in motivating others or demonstrating vision. We have developed our own training program and put about 200 people through training programs. We are very serious about change."

New Blood, New Values

National Australia Bank's Tredenick agrees that new blood is needed to bring about cultural transformation. "Culture change is of prime importance," she says. "It's tough, and takes a long period of time. But you have to change the symbols and the behaviors of the leaders. The values have to be visible."

She cites two examples of outdated values:

- People are promoted because they've been there a long time.
- Your voice is heard in the company because you have power.

"The CIO needs to personify the new values. People who perform should be promoted and rewarded. People should feel able to contribute regardless of their place in the organization," Tredenick says. "If you say you have an open door policy and are encouraging diversity, you have to mean it—and to demonstrate it."

Accenture's former Asia Pacific managing director, Jane Hemstritch, agrees that a new team at the top is critical if dramatic and effective change is to be achieved in an IT organization.

"The definition of stupidity is to do things the way you always did them and then to expect a different result," she says. "You can't expect people to suddenly do things in a different way. While religious conversions such as Saul on the road to Damascus are not unknown, they are rare. You usually do need to bring in someone new."

Hemstritch describes two stages to cultural transformation:

- Outline the vision.
- Work out who will support you in achieving it.

"The incoming or transformational CIO needs to look at the enterprise and what they need to achieve, consult widely and develop the vision and supporting set of values," she says. "They then need to hire new senior executives and quickly let go of others. If you don't, some of the people you don't want will wait you out."

Follow-through is also critical, according to Hemstritch. "It's no good saying things are going to be different, and this is what I want—and then not holding them to it. Often, CIOs can hang on to the wrong people simply because they have great technical skills. Those people will try to convince you that they only are the people who can do it. IT is especially vulnerable to not letting go of those people with the wrong behaviors."

Visibility and accountability are two key behaviors in successful transformations, Hemstritch says. "The incoming leader must see it through and be accountable. There must be consequences, or their credibility will be shot. There needs to be visibility, so that no one is under any illusions about what is needed."

Deloitte consulting partner Lisa Barry says cultural transformation is "the lifeblood of change." She outlines seven major fundamentals for change:

- Make your case for change.
- Have a clear vision.
- Develop a strategy.
- Work out how much organizational capacity there is to enact the change.

- Introduce strong motivation for change to the business.
- Communicate effectively: "Keep on top of the messages that are being transmitted through the organization."
- Be consistent in your own behavior: "Model the change that you are trying to make."

Transformation—Fast or Slow?

Transformational change is the catch-phrase of corporations as they reengineer business processes or product offerings to create sustainable competitive advantage. But change can be a slow process as executives face a minefield of obstacles.

As one executive interviewed by Heidrick & Struggles notes: "I don't know how many times I've heard that a transformation is happening. I see some quick wins happen, or some low-hanging fruit collected, but then the big picture never seems to emerge."

Singapore Media Development Authority CIO Chung Cheng Yeo believes technology change agents need to demonstrate a system or application that can deliver quick results before people will start to believe that beneficial change is possible. Yeo cites the case of new finance and human resources systems developed at the National Library of Singapore and then deployed at the Media Development Authority:

"Users said they had used their previous systems for umpteen years and they were quite happy with them. For their part, the technology guys asked 'Why should we buy a system when six engineers can build it in nine months?' My view is that you should try to avoid building something from scratch.

"It took us about nine months to actually install the systems and get them going, but once people began to see the benefits, one by one they got over their objections and are now looking at ways the new releases can help leverage the gains already made."

Four things to remember to become an effective change manager:

- Stick to your principles and focus on what changes are needed.
- Resist the temptation to get sucked back into making incremental rather than major change.
- Be resilient.
- Look for small successes and reward examples of excellence where you find it.

Former CIO Fran Dramis, who joined BellSouth in 1998 and retired when it was acquired by AT&T in 2007, introduced a change program that he describes as "a straightforward gap-analysis process." He compares the role of the transformational CIO to that of a captain in a yacht race.

"If the leader of the race is going 50 knots and your boat is only going 30 knots, you need to get more wind to the sails. A good captain will get the sail right to the point of ripping. That may only be 40 knots. But if someone says, 'I've got to get to 50 knots,' and they rip the sail, the boat stops and they'll never win. A good change agent stretches the culture to the point of disruption—but stops right before that."

He stresses one point: "Persuasion is the secret to moving up to competitive speed."

Starting Off Strong

In a leader's first days in a new role, results stem not from managing the business but from leading and listening to people.

Entering a senior management role presents many challenges. The performance measures are high and everyone will be watching closely. New leaders often feel pressured to start delivering results from day one. While money and improved profitability are the ultimate goal, new managers should remember that it is counterproductive to focus too intently on these issues—particularly in their early days. New managers should, rather, focus on the human elements needed for success: team morale, energy, passion, and ambition.

"What I often tell our young executives is to focus on the job at hand," says Kenneth Chenault, chairman and CEO of American Express. "While most people have ambitions, most do not follow through on 100 percent of their current commitments. (By following up on commitments, I mean to execute the assignment on hand.) Place yourself in the shoes of your boss, peers, and your subordinates so that you understand how to execute at your current level in order to make those people successful."

If everyone is successful, the business is successful, and this opens the door to promotion and growth. Making people successful, particularly a large team, involves a great deal more than merely wishing them well and delivering rousing pep talks. Typically, team members already know their jobs and what needs to be done—but they are not doing it to the best of their potential. Why? Countless causes affect people's behavior under these circumstances: natural wariness of change, lack of ambition, poor attitude, personal issues, or structural failures in the organization.

Most of these issues lie not in the realm of rational thought or intellect but in the realm of emotion and feeling. The role of a new leader therefore is to help people reach their full potential by subtly influencing their attitudes and feelings about work. Achieving this will ultimately result in happier people who perform better, which serves the ultimate goal of advancing the business.

FedEx's Smith is one of the world's most successful entrepreneurs, and a firm believer in the human touch. "If you aspire to run an organization consisting of a lot of regular folks, you're going to have to make an effort to get to know all of your people and understand how they think and feel about things," he says. "Employees in the trenches tend to have a more hands-on, practical knowledge of the business and are clear-headed—not theoretical—about the reality of how things work. Most senior executives today don't have enough contact at this level, and as a result are missing out on connecting with their constituencies and being better leaders because of it."

The key to adding value in the early days is to list areas where new senior managers ought to spend their time. Such a list is possibly endless, but each new manager should initially focus on a handful of areas that directly impact group morale and enthusiasm. Informal meetings with team members, celebrating individual and group achievements (both minor and major wins), and taking an interest in people's assignments (perhaps suggesting reassignment when it can help advance someone's career), are all extremely valuable ways to spend the early days in a new leadership role. When determining where to spend time, it is best to ask the following questions: What activities will raise enthusiasm and excitement? What activities do team members find most valuable? What activities does management expect?

Finally, it is crucial that new leaders clarify their relationship with their team, delineating items such as the leader's role, responsibilities, accountabilities, and performance measures. Surprisingly, this is rarely done in business. Leaders move into a new role and leave the evolution of their position up to circumstances and chance. Communicating clear guidelines early on helps to assuage any doubts the team members may have about a new leader, and it allows the leader to focus on the emotional areas from which the team's success will spring.

Here are the ways new executives add value early on:

- Spend informal time with team members, getting to know their role and coaching them.
- Get to know junior people, perhaps suggesting new roles or responsibilities to help add depth to their careers.
- Spend time following up with people, helping them achieve their objectives.
- Celebrate achievements, both major and minor.

Demonstrating Real Courage

The ability to influence others requires true integrity and an honest intellect. People can sniff out fakes. During tumultuous times, employees are keenly tuned to the moves of senior managers. They are looking for cues on how to act, clues as to what shape the business is in, and a sense of purpose to help keep fear from overwhelming action. In short, they are looking for courage.

Courage is not about being fearless. Nor is it about being the toughest. It is about acting in spite of fear. Moral courage. Not the courage that hides behind aggression, authority, or title. If you have been seen as an aggressive, bullying, socially withdrawn leader, that may have been fun during good times, but you'd be well-advised to remember that indulging in this kind of theater doesn't work when real leadership is demanded. There may come a time when your organization will be healthy enough again for you to entertain yourself with aggressive leadership behavior. But it is not this time. Employees and their managers need calm, focus, clarity, personal courage and real leadership.

Communicate; Create Clarity

The worst fear is nothing more than the unknown. A child is not frightened of the dark but of what the dark might harbor. Be honest with your people. Tell them what you do and don't know. Ask them for what they know. When you don't have anything to tell them, tell them that. Listen to those who need to communicate with you. Focus on what is important to them, not you. Don't gild your words now. Don't evade the issues or try to cushion them. Set up a blog to receive feedback and communication. Without the channels and intent for frequent clarity up and down, your organization is inventing false clarity. At times like these, all rumors are tinted with angst in order to justify the feeling of angst in the company in a clarity vacuum.

Make Imperfect Decisions

There is no time, need, or room now for the irrational quest for perfection that creates stalled momentum. Plan to make imperfect decisions to ensure that the factor of time is appropriately considered. The perfect decision does not exist. So how many more days or weeks should you add to the decision and analysis process to try to reach it? Momentum and activity toward progress are more important than the inertia of perfecting the plan.

No room for passive security needs here, either. Ensure momentum. Break inertia. If you have people with the drive to be making progressive decisions, then encourage this rather than testing and disqualifying them in your own insecure need for the one right answer.

Be Present; Be Seen

In a letter home after Waterloo, a foot guard reported that when his regiment had been decimated and only a few men stood to protect the colors on the line, they saw Wellington—"'Old Nosey' on his Grey"—just yards behind them through the smoke of battle. He had come forward to evaluate the situation before returning to the hill. In this moment, those remaining soldiers reported a surge in confidence and belief, and a desire to not let the old man down. They chose not to die that day. Not to indulge the French. They lasted until the reserves relieved them.

Though you yourself may be angry, depressed and confused, this is not the time to show such feelings. This is a time to get out among your people as much as you can. Answer their questions. Be seen to be approachable. Inject the whispering word of mouth yourself at multiple levels. People are looking for evidence to be alarmed. Don't let your distance or your countenance provide that evidence.

Don't Criticize

This is not the time to berate anyone for recent past mistakes or dwell on the myriad internal excuses that will be rising in you for "how we got into this mess." Keep your mind clearly focused on the future for your people. Offer them the opportunity to clean up for themselves. Recognize the opportunity to operate more efficiently, but get your people to define how. Set new goals but not new instructions. If the boom times have enabled management levels to take initiative and embrace freedom of action, then use this to solve current problems and avoid going back to solving their problems for them. Forgive those who falter initially. They are probably doing the best they can.

Manage Yourself: Set the Example and Find Examples

Get used to wearing some heavy "student driver" signs on your back again for a while. You are an impostor—you have told yourself this every day since the market changed. An army mantra for leadership in crisis reminds us that officers should never run, for it panics the men. Manage anxiety. Believe in yourself. Focus on the higher intent of the organization rather than the last dollar saved. Smile. Make time for people. Be made of Teflon. Seek feedback. Set up sentinels. Make time for selfish needs. Be available. Be personal. The use of the word *I* is less of a taboo in a crisis.

Be the colors—the rallying point in the smoke and noise of battle that assures your troops that hope prevails. Never let the colors fall. Apportion credit and take blame. Show that sacrifices are shared. Are you going to fly business class to visit one of your offices to tell them that they have to cut costs? Do you park among staff in a Mercedes?

Learn, Unlearn, Relearn

Make sure you are informed. Read. Read the newspapers. Read your company blog sites. Be a source of external knowledge and cling to the data that drives evidence for optimism. Reach out to other CEOs, sources of confidants and discreet support beyond your organization. Find someone you can share your concerns with who will not judge you and who will benefit in return.

So once more unto the breach, dear friends. There will come a day for giving up and indulging in self-misery and disengaging. But it is not this day. Not while you have faces around you who need to believe in you and find that spark of faith that rallies organizations and ensures that they stay high on the survivors' lists when history recalls the brave. While you have people with you, you must indeed keep your head while those about you are ready to lose theirs—and blame it on you.

True leadership at last has the chance to bloom in our privileged corporate universe. Leadership based on faith, purpose, and honor—and with courage at its heart.

Endnote

1 "The Gentle Art of Coaching," Heidrick & Struggles, May 2007. http://www.heidrick.com/NR/rdonlyres/FDC171D6-EFB3-48F8-9E50-E217ACAE9B18/0/HS_ArtOfCoaching.pdf

III
LEADING THE FUTURE

7

ENTER THE DRAGON: CHINA

Talent management is the single greatest problem that multinational companies—be they joint ventures or wholly owned foreign enterprises—face in China.

A CEO Challenge Survey covering 430 business leaders in China showed that 93 percent deemed the ability to attract, develop, and retain leadership teams their number one challenge (HIS/ Conference Board, 2004). CEOs and HR executives here have battled this issue on three distinct fronts:

- China's unique emerging market model
- The huge influence of multinational companies entering the market
- Increasingly aggressive local companies

In the battle over talent, CEOs and HR leaders are experimenting with a wide range of new approaches. Yet many of the solutions under discussion in China are not far from what companies employ in other markets. These priorities for staff development would sound familiar to any multinational operating anywhere in the world:

- Create a culture of top-down ownership of leadership development and succession planning.
- Invest in technology such as online assessment and other alternative approaches to identify and manage leadership talent.
- Create a talent management process that integrates both internal and external stakeholders (for example, business partners).

- Instill job performance, assessment, and development as core management processes.
- Make the company an "Employer of Choice" organization.

While elements of these are essential to create global parity in any multinational, tactics that work elsewhere cannot necessarily be shoehorned to fit the China scene. Talent problems in China are magnified by what McKinsey & Company refers to as the paradox of "shortage amongst plenty." In the *McKinsey Quarterly* (No. 4, 2005), Diana Farrell and Andrew J. Grant forecast that the demand for globally capable Chinese executives would reach 75,000 by 2008. The number of suitably qualified executives in 2003 was at best 5,000. Even if the talent pool grows at 30 percent per year, there would still be an enormous imbalance between supply and demand. Without an unforeseen and dramatic economic downturn in China, Heidrick & Struggles believes, this imbalance will continue for at least another 10 years.

Despite this talent shortage, most US and European multinationals that have entered the China market over the past 15 years use a talent management model that does not really apply in China.

This model reflects former GE CEO and chairman Jack Welch's view of the distribution of talent in an organization:

- Lead category: the top 20 percent of employees.
- Sustain category: the 70 percent of employees in the broad middle range.
- Remove: the lowest 10 percent of employees.

Under this model, a company will invest heavily in its top 20 percent (the company's future leaders), nurture its high-performing core management, and systematically fire and refresh its bottom 10 percent on a yearly basis.

This model worked extremely well for GE and has been adopted in different guises by global businesses as a way to retain a competitive edge. However, this model does not reflect the environment in China.

Two new classes of employees must be identified and evaluated when considering talent development in China, which we refer to as "potential" and "gray community" categories. The "potential" group is made up of employees who are intelligent, motivated, well-educated and ambitious, but lack the following key attributes:

- Business experience and professional maturity
- Emotional intelligence (EQ)

o Polish, poise and presentation with competent English skills
o Career management skills
o Effective role models and mentors

These employees are rough diamonds—executives who have the substance, intellect and desire to be successful, but who are easily overlooked because of their lack of polish. We think this category of Chinese employees is the most critical for businesses to build a high-caliber and sustainable leadership team in China. Recognizing this talent segmentation requires a talent development model that enables a company to identify this significant talent pool and provides a development, assessment, retention, and training program that is culturally in tune with the real situation in China—a critical step in creating a strong middle management foundation and future company leadership.

The second subclass we identified—the "gray community"—is just as important as the "potential" group. These executives exist in a "gray area" where performance is not clearly visible to the organization, often because firms do not have the tools or performance management systems to properly assess and manage this segment. Since multinational HR programs are based on a mature market model, it is difficult and even dangerous to make hasty decisions about performance.

The organizational structure may be flawed and job responsibilities ill defined, and training, development, and retention programs may not be culturally sensitive—all this makes performance difficult to measure. Cultural and economic factors can distort the assessments of an executive's performance. For example, an excellent manager in a small Chinese city may not meet business targets because of inflexible company policies or contract specifications—company practices that draw customers in Beijing and Shanghai won't necessarily work in rural China. The real problem may not be the manager but the lack of autonomy available on the job.

Proper and complete assessment of a company's talent pool is vital for competitiveness and survival in China. If business growth is 20 percent to 30 percent per year, yet one-fifth of company executives are hidden in a "gray zone" of competency, it's akin to a ship sailing in favorable conditions but dragging its anchor. Recently, 14 Asia Pacific and China CEOs were posed a question: "Based on your experience managing executives in China, do you think the level of performance is higher or lower in China compared to a mature market?"

Surprisingly, the collective view was this: they did not know. Many guessed there was a lower level of executive performance in China, but no one had quantifiable evidence either way. They reported that they did not have a clear view of performance across their executive talent pool, and that many HR departments were constrained by legacy evaluation systems applied to the corporation worldwide, which didn't always fit the China situation. In any case, firing low performers is counterintuitive in a market characterized by extremely high turnover—an average of between 17 and 20 percent a year.

Executives said there is almost an emotional block to cutting loose large numbers of low performers—with so many opportunities at other companies and nearly one-fifth of employees leaving each year, the GE-Welch system could be disastrous in an already difficult retention climate. The buffeting effects of market volatility, high attrition, and low executive supply have created a "perfect storm" for managing performance in China.

The reality of the workforce in China is that the Welch model is too limiting to be useful. In practice, talent falls into five brackets:

- Lead category: top five percent of employees.
- Sustain category: the next 20 percent of vital employees.
- Potential group: the middle 50 percent of employees earmarked for development.
- Gray community: the lower 20 percent, who should be evaluated for fit.
- Remove: the lowest five percent of employees.

Many multinationals' problems in China come from a lack of insight into China's emerging market model:

- Lack of bench strength in both the senior and middle management ranks.
- The lack of depth in core management ranks (particularly in the "lead" and "sustain" categories) explains the continued requirement for significant numbers of expatriate or local plus (foreign nationals on local payroll) employees from Europe, the United States, or other parts of Asia to make sure the business is run effectively.
- Chinese employees in the "sustain" category are often poached or considered for roles that they are not capable of performing. It is

the promotion of Chinese executives from the "sustain" to "lead" category that contributes heavily to overpaying and overtitling in China. The huge disparity between demand and supply for globally capable Chinese executives creates a market where Chinese executives are often paid 20 to 30 percent more than their counterparts in mature markets—even though the beneficiaries of this windfall in many cases only have 75 to 80 percent of the competencies their high positions require.

- Companies are struggling to create a solid mid-management "core" as they find it difficult to identify and buff the rough diamonds that exist in their own organization. This is the crucial "develop" category. If companies fail to deploy this crucial resource, they will not be able to deal with growth, attrition, deployment of new strategies, and leadership succession planning.
- Companies in China require a much better understanding of low performers. The first challenge for any company should be to evaluate their gray community of executives as either "potential" or "low performance."

Identify and Groom Local Leadership

In a dynamic and competitive market such as China, companies cannot afford to manage their business based on a mature market model any longer. Very few multinational companies understand the leadership demands in China, let alone tailor their HR programs and processes to the model that works here.

This lag in identifying and grooming talent is understandable—the breakneck speed of market changes leaves little time for proactive response. China's unprecedented economic growth has created huge volatility in its executive talent pool. HR talent that both understands local market needs and has the credibility within the company to advocate a change of corporate mind-set on this issue is in especially short supply.

Intellectual property is a cornerstone of financial success of any company, and corporations go to great lengths to safeguard their IP resources. Talent management—understanding and safeguarding the human capital IP that makes up a successful corporation—is the greatest intellectual property a company holds, and when well managed and deployed is a serious weapon to help best the competition.

The future of leading companies in China will be determined by the ability to find, groom, and hold on to talented diamonds in the rough, which will require a more sophisticated process of evaluating executives. Only then will companies fully reap the rewards of doing business in the world's fastest-growing economy.

Winning China's War for Talent

To win in China's war for talent, companies need to bring a strategic perspective to their hiring decisions.

As companies scramble to recruit in what will one day be the world's largest economy, they all too quickly relinquish the recruitment best practices they employ in more developed markets—much like an army abandoning a carefully laid plan at the first sign of the enemy.

Companies hiring in China also tend to have few measures in place to assess the efficacy of their recruitment process—save for the selected candidate's ultimate success or failure. Often collaboration between human resources and line management is weak, resulting in internal distrust and finger-pointing should a new hire fail to meet expectations. Line managers need to engage more in the hiring process, as opposed to seeing it as a job strictly for HR, and HR needs to be more proactive in anticipating the long-term talent needs of the organization, and in making a serious effort to partner with management.

Clear Recruitment Process

The first step HR departments can take is to set up a clear recruitment process. The process needs to lead all the way from the headcount plan and job description through the new hire's first year on the job. It needs to identify the source of the candidate (campus? competitors? another industry?) and then carefully screen applicants, a process in which both HR and line managers should work closely. When the point of decision arrives and the offer is ready, HR and line managers must work together to sell the proposal to the candidate. If the candidate spurns the offer, HR and line managers must work out the reasons for the rejection, and a clearly defined hiring process makes it easier to identify and resolve problems.

Leadership also needs to be prepared to sign off quickly on new candidates. The job market in China is extremely fast paced: quality candidates often have a range of career opportunities and may lack the patience to wait for a company that is dragging its feet. Repeatedly, companies have lost good candidates owing to either internal procrastination or the desire to see more candidates. In today's China, however, the adage "A bird in the hand is better than two in the bush" is highly relevant: if the right candidate is available, move forward as fast as possible.

Many companies are entering China hoping for a low-cost market, but have found that the limited pool of quality candidates means that costs in China's labor market are inflated. Candidates typically have a good sense of their market value, and companies must be willing to pay the price to get the right candidates. A number of variables affect the bargaining power of companies vis-à-vis candidates. But for experienced hires, companies should be prepared to offer an average pay raise of 20 percent and at least match the benefits of the candidate's current job.

Smaller Companies Can Succeed, Too

Money, however, is not always the first priority for candidates. In China, candidates are keenly interested in the individual managers with whom they will be working, as well as with their career prospects in an organization. In the area of career prospects, large brand name organizations have the edge when hiring, although smaller companies with less prominent brand names have been successfully hiring in China. But as a rule, smaller companies need to make a concerted effort to outline the opportunities in their specific line of business—which can be huge in China—and their commitment to the China market. They can be their own worst enemy, as they may take longer to decide on a candidate, likely resulting in the candidate deciding to go elsewhere.

All companies, both large and small, should have an on-boarding process and provide new recruits with an internal mentor. All too often, executive failure is related not to poor job performance but to a cultural misfit. Cultural misfit tends to be a bigger issue the higher up the corporate ladder one looks. In addition, if a company fails to take the longer-term view of nurturing a new employee and providing a clear career plan, the individual will soon leave.

In China's great war for talent, companies must adapt their best practices in hiring to the nuances of the China market. They must be flexible, act decisively when the right candidate appears, and have the right on-boarding programs and career opportunities to ensure a candidate's success. Most of all, they need to look to the years ahead and carefully determine the talent they need for the battles of tomorrow.

Managing China's Industrial Growth

The outlook for China's industrial category remains strong, with many pundits saying that China will continue to enjoy five to eight percent GDP growth rates annually over the next 10 to 20 years, provided there are no political disruptions. The slowdown in the United States and Europe could further add to industrial growth as hold-outs to outsourcing find few alternatives. This category encompasses a wide range of industries, including automobiles, aerospace, chemicals, and natural resources.

Traditionally, multinational corporations in these industries have viewed China as a low-cost manufacturing base for Western markets, but five years ago, this changed with the recognition of the China market's potential in its own right. Helping this trend is the tremendous improvement in China's transportation and technological infrastructure, not to mention high-profile power projects such as the Three Gorges dam.

This infrastructure boom in itself offers a huge market. Companies such as GE, ABB, Siemens, and Ingersoll-Rand have been selling a wide range of industrial products for capital-intensive infrastructure projects as the building boom has created a huge demand for products: turbines, fire alarms, intelligent building systems, lifts, specialty materials, control systems and electronics, to name a few. A massive industrial products market has opened up almost overnight.

The downside of this frenetic growth is the strain it has put on the market for top industrial managers. Ten years ago, companies were often led by Western expatriates. In the late 1990s, this changed, with 60 to 70 percent of top industrial management positions being filled by Asian expatriates. In the past two to three years, things changed yet again, with the focus now on returnee PRCs—Chinese nationals who have spent six to seven years working overseas. Given the tight market, however, Chinese nationals with 10 to 15 years of domestic executive experience (but no overseas experience) are also increasingly sought after.

Regardless of their background, top industrial managers in China find that the foremost prerequisite for progress is the ability to operate effectively in an international corporate matrix. Technical skills are readily available, but the leadership skills necessary to interact with multiple stakeholders at a main board level, and the ability to influence a global corporate agenda, are still X factors. Another key success variable for senior industrial executives is their ability to translate a global corporate agenda into an effective China strategy. They must be able to educate, modify, and reshape the often inaccurate views that home office executives may have of China, and at the same time create a frame of reference for Chinese government officials to better understand and deal with multinational corporations' concerns, issues, and requests. The ability to align different expectations in a commercially viable way is one of the most elusive leadership competencies in the China market today.

Reengineering Honeywell

Honeywell is a good example of a company that has been successful in identifying and developing this type of management talent in China. When Honeywell decided to consolidate its Asia Pacific headquarters in China and build a coordinated "Honeywell Inc." approach to its multiple businesses in the country, it required a new business model.

Honeywell spent considerable time thinking through the leadership skills required for this role and understanding the right mix of strategic consulting skills, industry experience, and market knowledge required to balance its global corporate strategy with the realities of the local market. The company carefully reviewed its corporate culture, and developed a benchmark of what attributes and behavioral competencies defined success for its people. It also reviewed past leadership models to determine which structures, reporting relationships, management responsibilities, and accountabilities were successful and which ones were not.

Ultimately, it developed a new leadership model that was a departure from anything it had used before: a model based on its unique corporate culture and on the specific needs of a culturally diverse and rapidly growing transitional market. It also undertook a realistic assessment of how this role interfaced with its traditional business unit structure.

Following this, Honeywell appointed an external executive, Shane Tedjarati. He had the right mix of entrepreneurial flair, deep China experience, and (most important) a proven ability to influence a global board agenda in the context of China. Furthermore, Tedjarati had experience establishing sophisticated frames of reference to help Chinese government officials and business leaders better understand legitimate multinational interests.

Given the insights Honeywell developed through its leadership review, it was also able to identify and attract an external executive who would not normally have made it onto the short list. To date,

Tedjarati has successfully facilitated step-change thinking in terms of Honeywell's complex business portfolio and is successfully working as a partner with strong business unit heads to link Honeywell's broad array of products and services to real opportunities in the China market. This approach has enabled Honeywell to establish a more significant market presence than it could have done had its individual business units pursued disparate strategies. This leadership model has created for Honeywell a competitively differentiated strategy for doing business in China.

Road Map for Success

To get China right from the leadership point of view, companies must first develop the correct strategy for acquiring, developing, and retaining leadership bench strength—and not just for top positions but for second-tier and middle-management ranks as well. Most companies, however, aren't structured properly even to do this, and most tend to delegate succession planning and talent development to their senior HR executives. Such companies must assume a more top-down approach to talent development.

The companies that have the best talent development strategies have formed internal steering committees, chaired by the CEO, that focus on leadership development strategies. The steering committee establishes the organization's leadership goals and holds management and HR accountable. As a further step, these steering committees are creating external advisory bodies with which they meet regularly. The advisory body offers external perspectives and ideas about best practices from noncompeting best-in-class organizations.

After establishing a steering committee, these companies usually conduct a gap analysis of their management ranks for the short and medium term. Following this, they establish what their key leadership needs are for the next 12, 24 and 36 months. They look at the best ways to develop talent through internal development, coaching, and training. In addition, once they have developed an understanding about where their real leadership gaps lie—as opposed to the reactive gaps that stem, for example, from an executive's departure—they need to enter the talent market to fill these mission-critical holes. This is a proactive, long-term, and, yes, expensive process, but companies prepared to follow this path will find their total costs over the years will be considerably lower than if they keep acting in what could be termed a more reactive, traditional manner.

Finally, a key challenge companies face in hiring the right executive in China is getting beyond culturally comfortable candidate attributes (such as a strong command of English) to more quantitatively assess a candidate's ability to represent the company's business effectively in China. If a candidate's communications and behavioral competencies appear less than acceptable to survive in an international matrix management culture, then the organization should develop these skills through training and coaching. This is a far better option than hiring somebody with excellent communications skills but not the core business competencies to meet the challenge of building and growing a sustainable business in a fast-changing, regionally diverse market.

One tool that is emerging as a useful predictive indicator of leadership potential is management assessment. Many companies are working with outside service providers to develop sophisticated assessment tools that provide alternative insights into a candidate's psyche, behavioral competencies, analytical skills, leadership style and values. Assessment provides an additional view of a candidate's potential to perform. However, the biggest criticism of management assessment to date is that these tests are based on a Western value system and have not yet been culturally adjusted to China in an academically accredited way. In addition, the assessment tool is often applied without tailoring the testing hypothesis and purpose of the test to the unique attributes of the company.

Therefore, at some point in the near future, there will be a real need for this type of management assessment, once these tests have been calibrated to the Chinese culture and the needs of cross-culture operating environments, and also tailored to the unique success benchmarks of the assessing companies. A holistic approach that assesses multiple quantitative and qualitative criteria, and that provides relative rankings against benchmarked success criteria for a specific company culture, will provide a more effective predictive tool for creating and developing winning teams. To date, no company is successfully doing this in China, as the tools have not yet been properly calibrated to the Chinese market.

As businesses evolve from international companies selling products into China to transnational companies that create, manufacture, and market China-specific products and services, the need for local yet globally qualified CEO talent will become increasingly pronounced. Given the scarcity of such individuals, companies will often be required to develop this talent in-house.

Companies will need to develop a culture of building winning teams first—otherwise most talent initiatives will be ad hoc and ultimately fail. Technology and alternative assessment methodologies will need to become a core process, driving every part of the company, including at least these areas:

- Developing a culture of building and retaining winning teams
- Fostering top-down ownership of leadership development
- Integrating multiple stakeholders (both internal and external)
- Redefining the role of HR as an asset manager and the key custodian of a company's culture of building winning teams
- Investing in technology and inserting alternative culturally attuned assessment methodologies into the corporate DNA
- Ensuring technology and assessment become core systems for the company—no point having superior senior managers if the rest of the organization cannot support their initiatives or is out of synch culturally with the management elite
- Developing innovative risk management strategies and processes for management development

The Cure for High Turnover in China

Keeping the current team happy is not just a matter of offering more money; it requires focusing on career development. This initiative to focus on people must come from the upper echelons of management. Talent must be identified and reviewed on a regular basis, and comprehensive talent development plans must be in place.

To succeed, a company needs to be perceived as a place where career development is an integral part of the culture. Successful companies distinguish themselves through more than their superior products and investments; they must also be seen to provide long-term careers and personal development opportunities, and to demonstrate their commitment to China.

"Commitment to China is demonstrated not only through investments but also by demonstrating a strong commitment to key talent consistently over a long time," says James Deng, CEO of Beijing Novartis Pharmaceuticals. Top managers at Novartis hold regular organizational talent reviews for the entire organization and select key individuals—referred to as *talents*—for a comprehensive development plan. Conditions and key milestones are communicated clearly, with progress reviewed on a quarterly basis. Selected talents go through comprehensive training and development programs tailored to individual needs.

Freddie Chow, HR director at Sanofi-Aventis, underlines the strategic importance of retention. "Building a stable team and retaining people is crucial to support our growth challenges," Chow says. "Our people understand our strategy, know our approach, and are very loyal. Losing our people is akin to losing our heritage and culture."

Sanofi-Aventis, the fastest-growing multinational in China over the last six quarters, has formed its own dedicated university, located in fixed premises with full-time faculty members working in cooperation with outside institutions.

The university's objective is to help Sanofi-Aventis remain the fastest-growing pharmaceutical company in China. To find sales managers, the company identifies management potential from day one through psychometric testing and other assessments, and in the last two years, the company has produced over 50 new line managers. The general market is aware that career development is taken very seriously at Sanofi-Aventis, making it easier to attract talent.

A substantial investment can be wiped out overnight when a talent departs, and many companies have devised schemes to ensure employees who depart soon after trips or training programs pay compensation. Relying on such handcuffs, however, often does not work. Chow says companies must maintain continuous dialogue and individual interaction with staff, sending the message that they are important.

The right compensation is, of course, essential. Only the very strongest companies can afford to compensate top talents at or below market levels. All others have little choice but to pay above market, particularly to attract top talent. To create incentives to stay, companies are increasing the variable rate of pay packages in the form of performance bonuses, and they are issuing stock options and restricted stock units that often vest years later. They offer cars with drivers, housing subsidies, executive MBA sponsorships, and savings plans. Packages incorporating these elements do encourage executives to stay, but rival companies are often willing to buy them out. While industry compensation surveys are important benchmarks, sometimes apples are not apples and it is critical to assess a talent's true value to the organization before pressing an individual into a predetermined compensation framework.

Finally, the companies that succeed in China's difficult talent market are those that are perceived internally and externally as strong at developing people, providing long-term growth opportunities, and demonstrating a consistent commitment to developing local staff. Retention of top talents is a long-term game. Setbacks can occur along the way, and there are no quick fixes. The winners in this game have a shared set of values and have created a strong company culture, shaped by a top team that is not subjected to regular international rotations. Retention stands and falls with a CEO's demonstrated commitment to create the best team through internal development. It is supported by a creative, persistent, pragmatic HR function that has a long-term and strategic outlook on how to sustain rapid growth amid a war for talent.

Battlefield Promotions

In today's war for talent in China, many executives are flying up the ranks and crossing from one industry to another. The phenomenon mainly exists in the key coastal cities where multinationals have their primary focus: Shanghai, Beijing, and Guangzhou. It is also starting to appear in key regional cities such as Dalian, Chengdu and Wuhan.

Twenty years ago, only a handful of foreign companies were established in China. At that time, multinationals filled their senior ranks with expatriates, but over the course of the 1990s, localization gathered steam, creating demand for indigenous Chinese leadership. At the same time, as various industry sectors opened in China, a flood of additional foreign companies started entering, all chasing the same small pool of talent. As local Chinese enterprises continue to develop and evolve, they too are joining the war for talent.

Back at home, multinationals tend to hire from within their industry. But in China, companies desperate for talent will target executives in completely different sectors. This stems from the fact that many key sectors are new to China. Retail, finance, and luxury goods are some of the more recent arrivals, and there simply are no seasoned professionals available. Companies' only recourse is to recruit from other sectors—particularly consumer goods—a mature sector by China's standards, with some 20 years of history.

Complicating things for China's human resources departments, anxious to hire and retain talent, is the ambitious nature of China's workforce. Top Chinese talents take career development very seriously and are acutely conscious of peer rivalry and status. Aside from competitive compensation, job titles and scope of responsibility are tremendously important symbols—and top talents are subjected to a never-ending stream of calls from corporate recruiters. The lack of mature professionals in many sectors, the flood of companies entering China, the need of companies to hire and retain talent, and the ambitions of top Chinese talent are all factors that contribute to the battlefield promotion phenomenon. Compared to their peers in mature markets, Chinese executives rise through the ranks much faster, in terms of both title and job scope. They spend shorter periods in a given position than their counterparts overseas before moving up, either with their firm or outside it.

While these executives have less time in market and are arguably less experienced than their Western counterparts, they have nonetheless earned their stripes. They have also developed different skills, owing to China's very different and dynamic market. China executives, for example, operate in an ambiguous market that is characterized by inconsistent infrastructure and consumer data points. It takes an innovative leader to assimilate significant regional differences in terms of products, pricing, people management, distribution, and manufacturing.

Such executives are highly effective, but from a Western point of view, they may seem unpolished. The challenge for a multinational is to recognize these individuals and then polish them. To return to the military analogy, such executives are like officers who have not attended a military academy but have been promoted based purely on their battlefield performance.

On the other hand, battlefield promotions can also lead to problems, as companies eager to attract and retain talent promote staff beyond their level of competence. Executives who have risen too fast simply may not have the experience to lead large teams in a challenging market, thus jeopardizing their career and their company's bottom line. What's more, such promotions can stoke internal rivalries: if one executive gets promoted, others will notice and begin looking for their own promotion.

Long-Term Career Paths

It is important for multinationals, particularly those contemplating an entry into China, to be aware of the battlefield promotion phenomenon and to develop the appropriate HR strategy to deal with it. First and foremost, overpromotion is not guaranteed to improve retention—at best, it is a quick fix to placate the ambitions of a top talent. Instead, companies should have clear long-term career paths for their top talent—often, such individuals depart because a career path has not been made clear to them.

Open communications and clear succession plans can be an invaluable tool when dealing with such talent. What's more, companies should resist the urge to promote certain individuals simply to retain them: They should instead help them develop the skills they require for the next stage of their career.

Talent development and retention is often more delicate than simply changing titles. Sandrine Zerbib, former president of Adidas Greater China, says that those who receive overpromotions often are individuals who have mastered hard skills over soft skills. Because soft skills take time, experience, and maturity to acquire, it is very important that companies identify top talent at an early stage, analyze what soft skills they are lacking, and help them develop those skills.

One well-tested way to help top talent develop is to rotate executives through headquarters for an extended period, six months to a few years. Such rotations should not be done merely for the sake of doing so, but should offer meaningful work experience, preferably in a new, challenging area that broadens an executive's career horizons. To make these rotations even more effective, Zerbib suggests giving top talent responsibility for a specific project that requires skills slightly beyond those they currently have, and ensuring they have a good mentor throughout the project's course. What's more, a career reentry point into the China market should be specified even before the executive departs—it is difficult to overstate how essential a clear career path is for Chinese talent.

As China continues to grow, the war for talent will continue to be fierce, and the phenomenon of battlefield promotions will continue apace. To retain top talent in the face of ever-larger titles and ever-bigger pay packages, it is critical that companies stay rational and outline clear career paths for their top talent. Top talents themselves should recognize the skills needed for career progression and resist the urge to constantly trade their way up the career ladder, a practice that could ultimately jeopardize their career. All wars end sooner or later, even wars for talent.

8

THE ELEPHANT IN THE ROOM: INDIA

India is changing the way the world works by improving the quality of its workers. But as the subcontinent moves toward becoming one of the largest economies in the world, many companies struggle to keep pace with the leadership skills required.

Multinational firms have long tapped India's intellectual capital, but its role as an outsourcing center with a deep talent pool has matured into a mighty market in its own right. The nation's growing ranks of competitive multinational firms are drawing not only top talent at home but a growing number of expatriate executives.

In October 2006, Carol Borghesi, a Canadian, was hired by India's leading mobile service provider Bharti Airtel to run its customer service business. Carol had a 26-year career in customer service, including a senior position with British Telecom (BT), but moved to India to be part of the fast-moving action here.

After working in Shanghai, Swedish national Marcus Wilhelm moved to Chennai in Tamil Nadu as COO, Photon Infotech. Compared to China, he says, India holds the edge when it comes to talent.

Many like Marcus and Borghesi have landed in the country to work. From a few hundred, expatriates' numbers have soared over the past five years.

Other names include Brooks Entwistle, managing director and CEO, Goldman Sachs (India) Securities; Trevor Bull, managing director, Tata AIG Life Insurance; Rob Hennin, VP and country manager, India, American Express Bank; Phil Nelson, VP, technology and back-office operations, AOL India; Jamie Heywood, deputy CEO, Virgin Mobile India; Andrew Davies, CFO, Vodafone Essar; Ertop Saltuk, VP, HR South Asia, Alcatel. The list goes on.

What is spurring companies to hire experienced expats? It is the demand for professionals with international experience combined with a shortage of top talent. India's strategic importance alone is sometimes sufficient to attract executives. As more Indian companies go global and more global firms target India as a strategic growth market, India's corporate sector is increasingly looking for people with global exposure who can handle complex businesses that blend both domestic and international operations.

Expatriates are filling the void created by the deep need in India for world-class managers. According to a recent survey, India currently needs more than 1,000 CEOs across industries, many of them in new sectors such as special economic zones, aviation, and airport management, as well as in media, communications, real estate, and retail.

The growing need for professionals with international experience, coupled with a shortage of top talent across sectors, is resulting in a dual approach for companies in terms of talent acquisition: attracting experienced expatriates to India and grooming talent from within organizations with an increased focus on staff development.

As India becomes an important part of the globalization strategy for many companies, several are relocating top executives to India. The goal is not just to oversee their operations in a strategic growth market but also to build and prepare a strong global team from India.

Cisco recently selected India as the site for its globalization center and relocated one of its top executives, chief globalization officer William Elfrink. Boeing recently appointed Ian Q.R. Thomas as vice president international and president of Boeing India, leading Boeing's enterprise-wide India team.

In a recent interview, Cisco's Elfrink said, "The country is more vibrant and adventurous in its pursuit of excellence than ever before, and our decision to locate our Globalization Center East in India definitely highlights the country's growing importance in the world. As chief globalization officer, I am responsible for implementing and overseeing a US$1.1 billion investment in India, executing on the growth strategy for Cisco globally."[1]

Cisco expects that in the next two to three years, every function in the company will have at least 20 percent of its top executives based in Bangalore.

"The market in India is a lot more than just selling commercial airplanes or defense products," says Boeing's Thomas. "I am here to lead a cross-enterprise team that goes beyond these two areas. We would like to partner with Indian business in a host of things such as IT, business process outsourcing, engineering, manufacturing and raw materials sourcing that the Boeing Company can bring to bear as an enterprise."[2]

One common stopgap measure has been to import knowledge and processes by seeding the human value chain from overseas or through strategic alliances and joint ventures. Reliance Industries, for instance, is reported to have over 100 expatriates in senior management at its retail division, while Bharti Enterprises benefits greatly from its joint venture with Wal-Mart Stores, the world's largest retailer. Sunil Bharti Mittal, chairman and group CEO, Bharti Enterprises, has even said that "Wal-Mart's global expertise in supply chain and logistics will bring enhanced efficiencies across the [entire local] retail ecosystem."

Looking ahead, India's retailers will need to build local bench strength through conscientious on-boarding, retention, and succession planning strategies. Expatriate leadership needs to be brought up to speed in terms of cultural, workplace, and market sensitivities. Where most foreign salaries range between US$500,000 and US$600,000, including perks and stock options, relying on foreign talent alone is not a viable long-term option.

With many Indian industries still at a nascent stage, standard processes typically lack the maturity and sophistication of developed markets. Gaps are also evident in the local retail talent pool. Loic Bygodt, a business consultant with 16 years of international retailing experience who is now working in India, says, "There is a wide divide between the very few senior executives with strong retail knowledge and middle management. There almost seems to be a lack of strong, rigorous professional discipline at that level. As competition gets even more intense in the future, it will be critical to instill a culture of excellence and performance across all levels of management."

But the role of top talent in India is maturing. As it grows, corporate India must invest in its top management, transforming company leaders from merely effective domestic managers into global business leaders.

Talent acquisition and talent development are not new to India. Companies such as Hindustan Lever Ltd., Citibank and Oberoi have been universities of talent. However, India needs to focus on leadership development more than ever before as the nation grows exponentially and aligns globally.

Many studies predict that India will be one of the main centers of economic growth for the next 15 years. Deutsche Bank's research on

Global Growth Centers 2020 estimates that India, Malaysia and China will be the growth stars of 2006–2020 based on four key drivers: population growth, investment, human capital and trade openness. The study also forecasts that India will become the third-largest economy by 2010, surpassing Japan.[3]

Fast-Growth Talent Gap

The IMD International Search and Consulting consortium estimates that India needs about 2.3 million professionals in key services sectors, such as IT and information technology enabled services by 2010, which will further fuel the demand for globally competent management professionals.

This gap has led many companies to provide extensive learning and development opportunities for talented executives, and to invest in a pipeline of future leaders within the organization. More and more companies are putting their middle management on a fast growth track to take leadership positions and are sending them overseas to gain international experience.

Wipro, for example, offers its "Strategic Leaders Program" to its top management. The aim is to help them build a global mind-set and learn international best practices in strategic planning. Infosys grooms future leaders through a meticulous process at the Infosys Leadership Institute. The company has identified 400 leaders on the basis of several parameters and has a three-tier mentoring process—with the Infosys Management Council (which consists of the company's board of directors) assigned as mentors for the first tier.

Hindustan Lever recently added *Hindustan* (as India is known in Hindi) to its name, which the company believes will provide the optimum balance between maintaining the heritage of the company and the synergies of global alignment with the corporate name of Unilever. It also hopes to attract and retain global talent for its India operations with this more international corporate image.

Another trend fueling India's need for globally competent executives is the growing appetite of the "Indian multinational." Many organizations, such as the Tata Group and Infosys, are exploring global acquisitions and partnerships. From January to May 2008, more than US$50 billion worth of equity deals were made in India, according to data from investment advisory Grant Thornton.[4]

Clearly, the talent gap in senior management positions in certain sectors will become too wide to be met through available talent at home. More and more Western expatriates are taking senior positions in India, often to meet the growing need for specialty skills in new sectors.

As companies grow and accumulate a strong and diverse pool of global talent, the role of top management teams will evolve in India, with equal emphasis on business growth and organization, and talent development. A clear differentiator for companies will be a management team that can successfully do this with a global perspective.

An excellent example of this is the leadership at Infosys. Murthy, the founder of Infosys Technologies, has not only successfully mentored the company toward becoming a true Indian multinational, he has also carefully invested in its human assets.

Cisco Systems' executive migration to India is aimed not only at leveraging Indian engineering talent but at building and implementing the company's globalization strategy. This only underlines the need for Indian companies to build strong top management teams with a global perspective.

The successful companies of the future are looking to build top management teams that not only have the right skill sets but who also have a strong global business and people vision. As Murthy of Infosys says, "Our assets walk out of the door each evening. We have to make sure that they come back the next morning."

Value Proposition Versus China

India is ahead of China in terms of the proportion of its population with tertiary education. According to the Institute for Management Development (IMD) *World Competitiveness Yearbook* for 2001, about eight percent of the Indian population aged from 25 to 34 years had attained some tertiary education, compared with five percent in China.

Another edge is the use of English as a lingua franca among Indians. The nation also has a large pool of skilled labor. According to IMD, India ranks among the top three of 30 nations in terms of the availability of skilled workforce. This means hiring or recruiting talent is not a problem. Social and cultural issues no longer have any impact on hiring patterns.

But challenges remain. The key problem faced by Indian managers in achieving global leadership positions is lack of exposure to global scale and best practices. Indian corporations have been inward looking and protected. Many are only now beginning to compete in the global marketplace. Managers lack the killing edge to make critical corporate decisions. Indian companies need to work with industry and governments to revamp the country's educational infrastructure to meet the rising demand for new skills. Future sourcing deals will require Indian companies to get a fair degree of sophistication not just in technological skills but also in business skills, commercial skills and the ability to work with different financial engagement models.

Going forward, most of the Indian companies that succeed will have a model that is reasonably well distributed between onsite and offshore operations, though they will have to learn how to handle a multicultural workforce well.

Next Outsourcing Wave: Moving Up the Value Chain

India ranks highly on the global radar screen as a sourcing hub. While the popular image of India has been of "IT sweatshops" moving low-value IT and business process outsourcing (BPO) jobs from the United States (and to a lesser extent, Europe) to the subcontinent, the image on the ground is different.

True, a majority of jobs taken offshore still exploit the cost arbitrage. But the tide is turning fast. This means the image of India just being a base for software developers and call centers is rapidly eroding. The next wave of outsourcing to India is going to be in the knowledge sector, exploiting India's vast pool of scientific and engineering talent. GE and Intel were quick to capitalize on the potential many years ago. GE's John F. Welch Technology Center in Bangalore is the company's largest such facility outside the United States. With a US$60 million investment, it employs 1,600 researchers and plans to raise the number to 2,400.

GE Plastics has a 300-member research team in India. Texas Instruments (TI) established its development center in Bangalore as early as 1985. In *Progressions: Global Pharmaceutical Report 2004,* Ernst & Young identified India as an emerging hub for collaborative and outsourced R&D. India's pool of trained chemists, excellent track record of innovation, and US Food and Drug Administration (FDA)-approved manufacturing facilities enable local players to offer significant benefits in the drug development process.

The best-known Indian R&D companies are in pharmaceuticals—Ranbaxy, Dr. Reddy's Labs, and Sun Pharma, among others.

The success of Indian pharma companies has led to several multinational corporations flooding the market to take advantage of India's prowess in process chemistry. More and more pharma companies are setting up clinical research organizations in India. Biotechnology is also heating up, with Biocon and Shanta Biotech leading the way. Kiran Mazumdar-Shaw, chairman and managing director of Biocon, is the new star of the Indian economy. The initial public offering of her biotechnology company has made Kiran the richest woman in India and R&D the hottest element of the Indian economy.

Offshoring in the financial services industry has taken off in a big way, with India accounting for four-fifths of the global market, a report has said. In the wake of the subprime housing loan implosion, more US financial firms are using India to perform high-end work like mortgage origination, equity research, and software product development. Reuters, the financial news and information provider, has outsourced editorial jobs to India to expand its news service output, in addition to the center it has in Bangalore for the collation of financial market data.[5]

There's no question India's vast talent pool, both technical and managerial, offers immense opportunities for multinationals to tap into. Companies such as Citicorp, Unilever, and PepsiCo have all hired Indian managers to head global positions, primarily because of the broad outlook and expertise many Indian executives possess. Many of India's talents come from the country's top management universities, and they are on par with the best from Harvard and other Western management institutes.

As the market shifts, Indian companies are realizing they need to adopt a strategic sourcing framework and focus on the business value of a deal, not just on cost and efficiency, to stay relevant in a fast-changing environment. Leading Indian companies like Infosys, Tata Consultancy Services, and Wipro have already started making inroads into the upper end of the consulting spectrum. Indian companies are unlikely to completely lose this cost advantage. Moving up the value chain does not mean that cost becomes less important.

Domestic Market Explodes

Besides its outsourcing prowess, India is making great strides as a market in its own right. Take for example India's retail sector—which is predicted to grow by 40 percent annually until 2011, when it should be worth more than US$400 billion.

From Lucknow to Chennai, India's retail market is certainly as dynamic as its growth forecasts. Backed by global and large local players, new retail outlets are opening weekly across the country. Bharti Wal-Mart's and Carrefour's newly approved cash-and-carry wholesale centers will soon join the likes of Metro's wholesale centers. Tesco will join India's string of supermarkets such as Reliance Fresh, FoodWorld, and Spencer's. Hypermarkets such as Star India Bazaar, Big Bazaar, HyperCity, Giants, Shoprite, or Reliance Mart are busy mapping out their territories. Add to these the single-brand or single-category outlets, luxury chains, department stores, and the thousands of mom-and-pop neighborhood stores, and you will get a sense of India's bubbling retail scene.

In this cauldron of activity, India's retailers need to avoid having their fingers burned. Disproportionately high real estate prices, poorly connected distribution networks, and a lack of modern supply chain logistics and skilled personnel, as well as an elementary regulatory system, are all potential hazards.

As a result, India's local retail players have yet to close the gap in efficiency when measured against global operational metrics. KPMG reports inventory turnover ratios range between four and 10 for most Indian retailers, compared to an average of 18 in the United States. Similarly, stock availability is about 5–15 percent in India, compared to 95 percent availability of all stock-keeping units on the retail shelves of global retailers.[6]

With some analysts predicting a market consolidation with the next five to eight years, India's retail leaders are best warned to fortify their talent strategies in the face of an imminent shakeout. Not only does this call for the urgent placement of experienced business leadership across every line of business and function, it also requires the shortening of learning curves across all lines of the organization.

With the exceptions of industry institutions such as Kishore Biyani (Future Group), B.S. Nagesh (Shoppers' Stop), and Noel Tata (Trent)—industry pioneers who have helped define Indian retail as we know it today—most leadership teams are made up of professionals who crossed over from mass consumer, advertising, and strong distribution-oriented businesses, and who require almost instantaneous initiation into both front- and back-end retail processes. These range from managing the customer's brand experience and merchandising to inventory control and cold-chain logistics. Local companies such as Reliance and the Future Group have had to resort to setting up customized training programs in-house or sponsoring training schools. This is particularly helpful for local senior executives from other sectors who need to get up to speed while still working full time in their new jobs.

Shadowing experienced executives from developed markets is another sound method for knowledge transfer. By surrounding expatriate CEOs such as Andrew Levermore (HyperCity Retail), Russell Berman (Aditya Birla Hypermarkets), and Andrew Denby (Aditya Birla Retail) with a pool of talented senior managers, local companies are building succession pipelines for their future executive teams.

Tailored compensation packages and retention bonuses are becoming more common to boost motivation, productivity, and talent retention. The Birla Group, which runs the retail chain More, offers employees retention bonuses from day one, while Spencer's Retail offers its management employee stock ownership plans for when the company eventually goes public.

Growing Pains for Professional Service Firms

Along with its outsourcing might and burgeoning domestic market, India has seen an increased demand for professional service firms to help multinational companies establish and build their business. But as Thomas J. DeLong, coauthor of *When Professionals Have to Lead* (Harvard Business School Press, 2007), says, "Professional service firms (PSFs) are being challenged like never before—by clients, associates, and the competition, just for starters. But old-style PSF leaders are not equipped to respond. In the past, the work of PSFs was a gentleman's game and now it's a blood sport." This is especially true in India.

India's stellar economic numbers may stave off any serious bloodletting by PSFs in the country as booming local businesses, particularly those in the infrastructure, retail and technology sectors, fuel demand for outsourced professional services. That doesn't mean PSFs are home free. They, in fact, face a different set of challenges.

"There is a war for talent across all levels. At the senior level, however, professional service firms are increasingly demanding that leaders demonstrate sophisticated client development skills, skills that are hard to find in this market," says Sangeeta Singh, executive director of human resources at KPMG India. "India's PSFs have traditionally relied on their brand names and reputations to win new clients, and are only just getting used to the idea of having to actively market their services. Another challenge is instilling a sense of accountability in client service teams, both toward the client and for the services provided. This is also a relatively young concept in India. The talent pool in India has much to learn from their global contemporaries."

In a report titled *Creating People Advantage: How to Address HR Challenges Worldwide Through 2015*, Boston Consulting Group states, "One of the main HR challenges that companies will face in managing globalization is making sure that the right people are in place in the right locations, and that there is effective and efficient cross-country and cross-cultural collaboration." This is especially true for Indian PSFs as they expand beyond their borders.

"In our ventures overseas, we have noticed that there is greater domain specialization in mature economies. Service providers are able to integrate their understanding of their clients' industries with their technical expertise, and so are able to provide more sophisticated solutions. This is lacking in India and something that we are addressing," said Pratik Kumar, executive vice president, human resources, brand and corporate communication at Wipro.

"Above all, our greatest challenge has been in keeping pace with the growth of our business into new geographies and new markets. At Wipro, we have 20,000 staff members who are based outside of India, comprising 40 nationalities across 42 countries. You need good leadership to manage multinational growth well; people who are able to quickly localize your business concepts and values, and transform those teams into 'Wipro' teams, no matter where they are based," Kumar adds. "We actively incubate and grow local leadership teams, while at the same time, we encourage them to see their careers with Wipro on a long-term, global basis."

Regardless of the various challenges that India's PSFs face, they will have to orchestrate well-tuned recruitment and retention strategies and to practice what they preach, so to speak. Keep the following principles in mind:

- *Be your firm's investment manager:* Invest resources in building a long-term strategy, and don't just punt on short-term efforts to capture growth.

  "I was trying to recruit someone to join Arthur Andersen in the 1990s, and instead of saying yes or no, he asked, 'Do you think you can create an organization as effective as the one you head today?' I kept thinking about that challenge for a long time after he had left my room," says Ashok Wadhwa, who used to lead what is recognized as one of the front-running investment banks in India. "A small team and I ventured out to build a firm that could be regarded as a trusted adviser for clients. When we founded Ambit Corporate Finance and RSM & Co in 1997, we [wanted] to be one of the best professional services firms in India."

- *Be your firm's management consultant:* Carefully plan all the different aspects of the firm's growth strategy in relation to its talent needs.

  "Look at the long-term success factors for your organization in the next two to three years' time, and then start to build your leadership bench now. The environment is changing so fast that firms cannot afford to take a reactionary approach. They must be nimble and have a strong ability to adapt," says Kumar of Wipro. "Trawl the world for best practices and customize them to local needs."

- *Be your firm's public relations executive:* Communicate and rally enthusiasm for the firm's vision.

  "Ensuring good communication is absolutely vital. We have been investing in technology that allows our people to reach out to each other. Other than Wipro forums and blogs that solicit participation from people around the world, our leadership also spends time in our overseas offices for a period of about one month every year, in meet and greet sessions with local employees," continues Kumar. "We want to ensure that our people feel anchored locally, and yet at the same time feel like they belong to a larger global organization."

On the Migration Path Home

Firms across the globe have been echoing the same tune: India is where the action is. The country has been described by the president and CEO of Cisco Systems, John Chambers, as "a major force in the global economy" and by the chairman of Intel Corporation, Craig Barrett, as "one of the world's leading technology centers."

Multinationals have made great strides in India, thanks in no small part to overseas Indian nationals who have returned to head operations there, otherwise known as *returnees*. Companies captained by returnees such as Accenture, the Cisco Intel Alliance, and AMD have witnessed revenue growth that is hard to match elsewhere in Asia—or even in the world.

As India increasingly becomes a key global player with its enormous pool of talented workers, sophisticated technical capabilities, and growing domestic markets, penetrating knowledge about India and the skills to work effectively with Indian counterparts are now indispensable for senior executives in India. There is a growing demand for senior-level returnees in Delhi, Bangalore, Chennai and Hyderabad. Microsoft, which has six business units in India, has brought in three Indian returnees to take on country manager roles.

Most popular are Indians who have cut their teeth at product technology firms in Silicon Valley. With their experience in managing rapidly globalizing companies during the technology boom in the 1990s, they have the right skills to manage growth and build high-performance teams with a global mind-set for their Indian employers.

Having familial roots in India, these executives also bring with them a keen understanding of the local culture as well as a longer-term focus than other expatriates. They are, on one hand, more empathetic toward the local way of doing things, and on the other, more aggressive in driving growth and change where necessary. For internal transfers, returnees would have built a valuable global internal network and insight into how things get done between international offices, which in turn helps them keep Indian interests high on the global board agenda.

Several India country heads, such as Rajiv Nair of Autodesk, Ajay Marathe of AMD and Rangu Salgame from Cisco are high-profile examples of such returnees. Typically between 35 and 45 years old, returnees are often given the opportunity to build a higher profile than they would if they were to remain overseas, and view the India experience as a critical part of their résumés.

With salaries approximately on par with their American counterparts, they enjoy higher purchasing power in India, where housing, for example, can cost significantly less. Returnee pay packages often include allowances for housing, cars, return trips, and educational tours within India. By returning to their roots, returnees may leave behind independent college-aged children, or bring with them young children to whom they would like to provide the "India experience." To ease the transition for their families, it is not uncommon for companies to offer assistance with locating schools and domestic help.

Returnees also bring inside knowledge of global supply chains and vendors, and a large global network of clients—especially in the banking, financial services, and insurance domain. Examples include Don Price, chief technology officer, and Tina Uniken, chief marketing officer, at Bharti Televentures; Scott Bayman at GE; and Baru Rao, CEO of Cap Gemini in Mumbai.

R2I Defined

On the surface, they may all seem very similar, but India's returnee professionals are anything but homogenous. Here are the categories of return-to-India (R2I) individuals that usually make it to the candidate short list, according to employers in India:

- *Fast trackers:* Executives who started their careers in India before being promoted to regional roles outside India or to more senior roles in other countries.
- *Transferees:* Executives already working in India on expatriate packages, having been transferred or seconded to their employer's Indian subsidiary or joint venture on short-term contracts lasting three to five years, or on permanent contracts.
- *Emerging managers:* Professionals in their mid-20s or early 30s who come armed with prestigious academic qualifications from the United States or Europe.
- *Domain experts:* Indians with an international track record in industries that are now expanding at home, such as real estate, clean-tech investing, and finance.
- *Relationship networkers:* A relatively small group, relationship networkers cover the Indian market from overseas, such as a private banker covering the Indian market from Singapore, Hong Kong, or Dubai.

While returnees are often expected to hit the ground running, it should not be taken for granted that they will escape the challenges in cultural assimilation that foreigners face. This is especially true for those who have been away for 10 years or more. Other than the need to get used to a less sophisticated infrastructure in India, there is also the slower pace of decision making, a greater number of government hoops to jump through, and the greater deference to hierarchy. The Indian work environment is still not as quick-action-oriented as that of the West, and its workers tend to be more grade- or title-oriented. Returnees therefore need to adjust their leadership styles to be more compatible with internal culture, and actively delegate with clear mandates for delivery to local staff.

Companies too could do more. In addition to the usual aspects of orientation, where returnees are given the company's operating plans, strategic plans, organization charts and important presentations, companies could make better efforts to include insights into the informal aspects of returnees' roles. These include tips on how decisions are made internally, how to gain support for initiatives, what cultural idiosyncrasies exist and how to work with the local and national government bodies.

In an increasingly global and networked workplace, there will soon be a seamless talent pool between the United States and regional centers such as India. By building their credentials in India, returnees will be well-poised for the next jump up the corporate ladder to global management.

Endnotes

1 "Globalizing India's Leadership," Heidrick & Struggles, September 2008. http://www.heidrick.com/NR/rdonlyres/66D61AC1-906E-4058-9D03-10F66700DE98/0/GlobalizingIndiaLeadership.pdf
2 Ibid.
3 "India: Beyond Cost Arbitrage," Heidrick & Struggles, October 2006. http://www.heidrick.com/NR/rdonlyres/2A922391-D087-4950-B0B4-D7720DD3AC66/0/HS_ IndiaBeyondCostArbitrage.pdf
4 "Do You Have the Right Leadership for India Inc.?", Heidrick & Struggles, July 2007. http://www.heidrick.com/NR/rdonlyres/A8EC1697-65EA-4921-932D-2DA96596FBD3/0/HS_LeadershipforIndiaInc.pdf
5 Ibid.
6 "India Retail Bubbling Over," Heidrick & Struggles, March 2008. http://www.heidrick.com/NR/rdonlyres/0AFFCDB8-EEB8-4495-84A6-2B7CF5A60FC2/0/HS_IndiaRetailBubblingOver.pdf

9

THE FUTURE OF BUSINESS LEADERSHIP IN ASIA PACIFIC

Imagine how life will be for future business leaders in Asia Pacific...

Soothsaying is a risky business. The future is difficult to forecast—imagine the reception one would have had 25 years ago touting the imminent fall of the Berlin Wall or the proliferation of personal computers able to communicate instantly across the planet for pennies. Sometimes, however, prognosticators get it right. Lafcadio Hearn, an American journalist who traveled and lived in Japan, predicted in his 1894 book *The Future of the Far East* that once cheap, plentiful labor met Western industrial and commercial practices, the region's economic power could take on the world.

A century later, Hearn's prediction is coming to pass. For example, the influx of outside investment in China alone has created the world's largest pool of foreign reserve funds, which surpassed US$1.7 trillion in April 2008 (and now growing at the mind-bending rate of US$10 million per hour, according to a recent article). What will happen next?

In this chapter, we first conjure up a picture of an executive in China and see what issues the generation now entering their teens may well be facing a quarter century from now, both in China and across Asia Pacific. Then we turn to innovation and charity, two areas likely to shape the future of the region.

The Coming Chinese Diaspora

Shenzhen, China; the Year 2030

David Wu sits at his window of his high-rise apartment in Shenzhen, weighing his options. The 35-year-old holds a photo of his grandfather, taken in the late 1960s when he worked the rice fields near this once-rural town. His grandfather stands at the center of a group of other villagers, clad in his Mao suit, clasping a copy of the Great Leader's Red Book. The scene could have been captured a thousand years ago, thinks Wu—a Wharton graduate who has quickly climbed through the ranks of several leading Chinese multinationals.

He stares out the window at the surrounding skyscrapers—hard to believe that this city, edging toward a population of 15 million, is the same place where the shot was snapped. But just now, he is not thinking of Shenzhen—he is thinking of Sydney, Atlanta, and San Francisco, places where prospective employers are dangling attractive expatriate packages for him to relocate.

Leaving his ancestral home isn't what makes him pause—after all, Chinese have been leaving these shores in search of brighter futures for years. But unlike the past diasporas, where poor economic conditions pushed Chinese abroad, it is now easy for executives like Wu to carve out a solid future in China. He already has a beautiful apartment, a helper for his wife and son, a BMW in the parking garage. No, unlike the immigrants of old, he is being pulled away with tantalizing visions of wider spaces, better hours, and mornings where clear sunlight—not this everlasting brown overcast—is the first thing seen through the window.

On the mantel are pictures of his father—these pictures are really the only childhood memories of his father he has. While he remembers countless hours at the knee of his doting grandfather, he has scant recall of his father—always traveling, always away. Among the pictures are shots of his own son, now five—what choice is best for him? That is the real question. He thinks of the cutthroat competition to get his son into the city's best preschool—a preview of things to come. (There was a story on the local news tonight about the alarming rise in teenage suicide—university entrance exams to blame. It was followed by a piece on the city's record crime rate.) He doesn't want his son's childhood memories of him to be the sound of a door closing in the early morning and reopening late at night.

> On a notebook, he writes: "private school tuition and placement," "paid home visits," and "six weeks' vacation" and heads to his computer to send his response to the corporate recruiters. He is curious to see who will be the first to accept his terms.

Executives: The Next Wave of Chinese Exports

China's economy has grown enormously in the past 20 years, eclipsing Great Britain as the world's fourth-largest economy by GDP (and second only to the United States in GDP purchasing power parity). Many economists believe China is on track to be the world's largest total economy by 2030, when David Wu (the fictional executive in our example) is considering his career options.

Based on a number of prevailing trends, China as a world-leading economy will be very different from the record-breaking developing market we see today. Besides cheap labor and goods, China's most valuable resource for multinational corporations in the future will be its swelling pool of executive talent. China's emergence as the world's greatest source for corporate talent will prove as explosive as its first-wave juggernaut as a manufacturing titan for the world economy.

China is uniquely positioned among emerging markets to respond to market forces and churn out future business leaders as it does products. Heidrick & Struggles research runs counter to present concerns about China's paradoxical "shortage in the land of plenty" in the search for global executives here. Farrell and Grant's an oft-quoted 2005 McKinsey and Company study estimates that only a small fraction of Chinese executives—about 10 percent—have the skills and experience necessary to work for a foreign or domestic multinational company, creating a shortfall of some 70,000 qualified executives in China. For example, the report points to China's engineering graduates, estimated to be 1.6 million—more than any other country McKinsey examined. According to the study, one-third of Chinese students study engineering, versus 20 percent in Germany and just four percent in India. However, McKinsey estimates that only 10 percent of these graduates were—by education and experience—on par with engineering students in developed markets. By dropping the numbers qualified to work at multinationals from 1.6 million to 160,000, the number of suitable engineers is no larger than that of the United Kingdom.

While that picture may be an accurate snapshot of 2005, advances in China's education are happening as rapidly as in the rest of its economy. Because of the scale of China's population of 1.3 billion, even modest improvements make substantial differences. Raise the ratio of internationally qualified engineers from one-tenth to just one-third of all graduates, and China would have the world's largest talent pool of globally capable engineers.

A recent study by Heidrick & Struggles and the Economist Intelligence Unit, mapping global talent in 30 major markets across the world, shows that China is making great strides in this direction. By examining each market's natural potential for producing talent in sociodemographic terms, as well as conditions necessary to realize this potential—such as demographics, quality of compulsory education, quality of universities and schools, quality of environment to nurture talent, mobility of labor, and market openness—China rated in the top eight out of the 30 countries studied. Forecasting current trends out to 2012, China will crack the top six. This is a remarkable achievement, considering most global leadership talent is likely to be found in developed, wealthy economies.

That a developing market's talent pool is leaping ahead of world-class economies such as Japan speaks more to the rapid improvement of future talent indicators in China—such as burgeoning enrollment at secondary schools and improvement of university programs—than to the erosion of standards in developed markets. For example, the joint Hong Kong University of Science and Technology–Kellogg School of Management at Northwestern University executive MBA program—which draws a third of its students from mainland China—was created only a decade ago, but last year was listed as the best program globally by the *Financial Times* annual ranking (a joint program of Washington University and Fudan University in Shanghai, created six years ago, was ranked seventh). A proliferation of similar programs—such as the new MIT–Shanghai Jiao Tong University program—augurs well for the exponential improvement of management talent in the next decade. The quick success of these globe-trotting programs speaks volumes about the extraordinary business leadership pool in the market where they are based.

By the Numbers: The Silver Tsunami

Demographics is the most reliable predictor of what the near future holds. Unlike technological political and financial market upheavals, demographics takes a generation to change its course. Across the developed world, a huge iceberg looms ahead.

The Baby Boomer (born 1946 to 1964) generation will begin to hit retirement age (65) in 2011. In wave after wave over the next two decades, this generation will leave the workforce—the last tide leaving the office in 2029. We will likely see mandatory retirement ages edge upward, but this will be a mere Band-Aid fix—mortality rates and age will do their work well. The chasm created by replacement workforce issues will grow into a canyon.

In the United States alone, "70 million baby boomers will retire in the next 15 years—only 15 million new workers will replace them," according to a 2008 report by Deloitte Research presented at the Asia Pacific Council meeting, May 28, 2008. "The 'silver tsunami' will cost some companies more than half of their senior leaders," the study says. Already, the impact of this seismic change is being felt. Over 75 percent of global companies say the lack of executive talent and their organization's inability to develop future leaders is a critical concern, according to *the 2008 IBM Global Human Capital Study.*

Part of this is the result of the rise of global affluence, which lowers per capita population growth. The developed world and developing giants like China are also benefiting from the greatest era of peace the modern world has known. Although conflicts in Iraq and Afghanistan—and the post-9/11 anxiety of terrorism—make this seem counterintuitive, it's a statistical fact. As *Newsweek* editor Fareed Zakaria recently pointed out, global trends have "created an international climate of unprecedented peace and prosperity... wars of all kinds have been declining since the mid-1980s and ... we are now at the lowest levels of global violence since the 1950s."

This new era devoid of major international conflicts is driving economies upward and populations downward. It is also increasing the mobility of workforce across country lines. The decline of military conflicts will stoke the global war for talent in unprecedented ways, as multinational companies are forced to look further afield to find future leaders.

Where Will They Find Them? China

China will become the central theater of the global talent war because it is already becoming a do-or-die market for most multinational firms. Twin forces will inevitably lead the search for qualified executives in the next generation to China: workforce deficits in Europe (anticipated to be 100 million) and the United States (between 25 million and 40 million), and the globalization of Western companies. A simple analysis of the top 20 Fortune 500 companies showed their global revenues increasing from around 17 percent in 1997 to 32 percent in 2007—mirroring the explosive economic growth of China. By 2025, we postulate this will reach 50 percent for most of these companies. The rising domestic consumption power of China (with a middle class of 300 million—equal to the entire population of the United States) will create a market unequaled in the world, one that will decide the future winners and losers among multinational corporations. With such importance placed on it, China is destined to become the major poaching ground for the executive suites of multinationals around the world.

In taking on the world, China already has a head start—its people are already there. The number of ethnic Chinese worldwide is conservatively estimated at 40 million—double the population of Australia and two-thirds the size of the United Kingdom. The Olympics illustrates this phenomenon, as world attention moves from the Summer Games in Beijing (the capital of China) to the 2010 Winter Games in Vancouver, Canada (where one of every five residents is Chinese). History and unique facets of Chinese culture have forged a global community that transcends religious, cultural, and geographic boundaries. As seen in the Beijing Olympics torch relay protests around the world, the Chinese are tight-knit when challenged. This sense of identity has created the world's largest business network: invisible, highly networked, and exclusive. They have cut a path that future Chinese executives will follow.

The Next Generation: New Goals, New Values

But as China changes, so changes the next generation of corporate executives. Our fictional David Wu—who would be 13 years old in 2008—lives in a vastly different China from that of his father and grandfather, with quickly changing values. The Generation Y of Chinese youth—like their counterparts across the world—are tech-savvy, more interested in career than company loyalty, and place as high a value on lifestyle as they do on livelihood.

Here is where foreign multinational firms will have an edge attracting Chinese executives abroad. By the time our David Wu is 30 years old, more than 220 cities will have populations of one million or more (compared to 35 today in Europe), according to the McKinsey Global Institute. More than 40,000 skyscrapers will have been constructed in

China by 2025—the equivalent of 10 New York City's worth of buildings—as two-thirds of its population shift to cities.

This massive rush toward urbanization will have a variety of lifestyle implications. China is already home to 16 of the world's top 20 polluted cities, according to *The Economist*—and it's hard to fathom that China's growing environmental conscientiousness will keep pace with this rapid period of construction. As cities grow, so will competition in Chinese schools—from preschool to university. If crowded, dirty cities aren't enough to drive young executives abroad, sex may become a powerful driver. Thanks to the success of the "one-child" policy and cultural preferences for male children, young Chinese men will grow up with an unprecedented shortage of potential brides. About 120 boys are born for every 100 girls today, in what the *Los Angeles Times* labels "the worst gender imbalance in human history... within five years, the country may have 30 million men who cannot find wives." Studies show that young single men are far more likely to commit violence than their married peers, exacerbating the growing crime rates that urbanization inevitably brings.

For the current executive class from the Baby Boomer and Generation X crowd, materialism is the unifying mantra. Most were born into perceived poverty—an "iron rice bowl" environment with state-set income levels. The mercantile class, while wealthy, was not respected.

Today, economics has changed all that. Since Deng Xiaoping, the architect of China's economic reform, uttered the words "to get rich is glorious," a void in any moral and ethical system created an ultracompetitive, get-rich-quick mind-set where the end justifies the means. Accumulation of wealth became the key measure of success—the fact that it is at other people's expense, damaging to the environment, illegally obtained, or unethical is irrelevant. The massive skews in wealth between the haves and have-nots—and the potential social instability this will create—is lost on this generation, who have grown up in a dog-eat-dog environment.

However, the next generation will see it differently. They will grow up in an era of reasonable affluence, but will suffer from overcrowding, respiratory illness, and ultracompetitive school systems. They will question a corrupt business environment that does not reward based on merit. As the Communist Party and strident nationalism become less relevant to their daily lives—even contrary to their needs—they will look for a more meaningful value system. This "green" generation will value things such as health, environmental quality, balanced education, access to green space, personal space and a place where their children can grow up in relative security.

As China morphs into the world's largest megalopolis—with increasing crime, ecological disasters, food shortages, and heated competition for basic services such as education and medical care—this group of executives will be tempted like never before to pursue career opportunities in those markets that can offer a respite from China 2030.

The landscape of China 2030 isn't a distant concern—the forces that will create it are in play now. As survey after survey shows, company leaders worldwide already rank the lack of qualified managers as a top concern—within the next decade, that "concern" will turn to "crisis."

Qualified, bilingual Chinese executives like our Wu will have their pick of global opportunities over the next decade and beyond. In a role reversal, we will see multinational firms offering extravagant expatriate packages to Chinese executives willing to relocate their families abroad. Mature markets in the West will need to modify immigration policy, tax incentives, and market access to meet the huge workforce deficit they face. China is creating the world's greatest pipeline for young global leadership talent. According to a study by Cass Business School in London (reported September 1, 2007), China's CEOs are on average 10 years younger than Western CEOs and 20 years younger than Japanese executives. But Chinese companies will have a fight on their hands to hold on to their talent, as nationalism and cultural connection will lose their grip on keeping them at home. Domestic multinationals will need to mirror the best practices of competitors abroad—including changes in company philosophy on the environment and human resources—to keep future executives close to home, or face one of the greatest brain drains in history.

The dawn of the Chinese executive diaspora is upon us.

Innovation and Asia's Future Business Leaders

The role of business in the world at large has expanded in recent decades. Stakeholders in the future of a business—be they employees, stockholders, clients, or customers—demand that leaders of corporations be good stewards for the communities they serve, not just for the bottom line. With increased pressures for transparency in business—coupled with the 24/7 pervasiveness of media and the desktop digital power of pressure groups to reach a global audience—actions of businesses and their leaders are facing unprecedented scrutiny. Reputations of executives and the companies they serve are at constant risk.

This has led to a convergence of shared values between the business community and groups that traditionally have been at odds with large corporations. Corporations are working hand in hand with community groups to address issues such as global warming, water conservation, recycling and energy efficiency. This is especially true in developing countries in Asia Pacific, where rapid advances in industry are putting pressure on natural resources and affecting everything from the price of commodities to the wellness of citizens in burgeoning industrial centers.

In this dynamic environment, company leaders are finding innovative ways to achieve the goals of growing market share, reducing costs and increasing a company's standing as a responsible corporate player in the communities it serves. In recent years, Heidrick & Struggles has partnered with the Asia Society to host conferences that bring together the best and brightest leaders from business, government, and non-profit organizations to examine the issues that will shape the landscape of Asia in coming decades.

At the 2008 Asia 21 Young Leaders Summit in Tokyo, where Heidrick & Struggles was a knowledge partner, nearly one-third (32 percent) of the respondents to a survey considered "confidence in financial markets" to be the top global challenge for 2009. For 23 percent, the priority challenge was "inspiring a shared vision."

People and innovation were cited as key success factors in the survey. An effective leadership team was top priority, followed by an innovative culture and highly qualified talent. Four out of 10 respondents considered "encouraging employee initiative" as the best way to foster innovation in organizations.

In summary, the advice from the next-generation leaders gathered in Tokyo was:

- Be true to yourself and your convictions
- Follow your vision and don't lose sight of your dreams
- Value your team and people

The shift of Asia's future business leaders toward concerns of community can be seen in this survey taken by Heidrick & Struggles at the 2007 Asia 21 Young Leaders Conference in Singapore.[1] A poll of half the 300 delegates shows these key findings:

1. Overall, poverty and uneven economic development are seen as the predominant challenge facing the Asia Pacific region (52 percent),

followed by insufficient governance (14 percent) and environmental concerns (pollution and climate change 12 percent).

2. The three top competencies considered important for leaders today are also the top three chosen for future leaders:

    a. Mission, vision and values (41 percent)

    b. Communication and interpersonal skills (19 percent)

    c. Problem solving (17 percent)

3. People-management skills are important. The highest-ranked task of leaders is to bring people of different talents and backgrounds together to achieve a common goal (46 percent).

4. Reflecting the personal values of the summit delegates, integrity (24 percent) and commitment (17 percent) were highly ranked as important leadership values, followed by teamwork (13 percent) and concern for others (10 percent).

5. The most common pieces of advice for next generation leaders:

    a. Follow your vision.

    b. Be true to yourself.

    c. Have empathy and hone your people-management skills.

Caring for the community was also notable at the 18th Asian Corporate Conference in Tianjin, China, in 2008. The Asia Society and Heidrick & Struggles brought together business and government leaders from around Asia for a discussion that centered on innovation and sustainable development in the region. Interviews with 55 senior business delegates from top international companies showed that innovation and environmentalism are growing hand in hand to improve business practices in the region.

Some key findings from those interviewed:

1. Many business leaders acknowledge that environmentally conscious investments can lead to commercial profits (63 percent), although 31 percent see such investments as having no financial impact.

2. All the respondents agreed that being a leader in environmental sustainability would improve their brand image and reputation (100 percent), as well as have an impact on areas such as these:

    a. Improved competitiveness and market positioning (89 percent)

    b. Employee recruitment, motivation, and retention (88 percent)

    c. Improved investor relations and access to capital (81 percent)

3. Innovation is seen as key in promoting environmental sustainability in companies' corporate goals, either through managing the environment (34 percent) or as a driver of environmental sustainability in general (26 percent).
4. A corporate culture that fosters innovation is seen as having an impact across the board, on areas such as these:
   a. Long-term growth (98 percent)
   b. Leadership development (98 percent)
   c. Employee morale (96 percent)
5. Innovation is encouraged across all functions, especially in business strategy and planning (18 percent), knowledge and improvement (15 percent), sales, marketing, and customer service (12 percent), environment, health, and safety (11 percent) and leadership coaching, retention, and development (10 percent).
6. Encouraging employee initiative (45 percent) is seen as the main driver for fostering innovation, followed by financial incentives (20 percent).
7. On the other hand, sharing and applying expertise across the organization is seen as the main hurdle to fostering innovation (37 percent), followed by aligning implementation with market demands (27 percent).

Sustainable Growth, the Environment, and Innovation

Rapid economic growth without proper regulatory controls has caused severe environmental problems in Asia, particularly in China and India. With the Olympics in Beijing, China has made a great effort in cutting down pollution—but it still has a long way to go. While there is a temptation to point fingers at China and India, even Western cities like Pittsburgh and Los Angeles went through a similar phase when they were first developing. China and India, however, are under increased scrutiny because of their sheer size and emergence at a time where greenhouse gas emissions are a global concern.

The city of Tianjin knows firsthand the problems of sustainable development. Huang Xingguo, mayor of Tianjin Municipal People's Government, says the province's pressing development issues include water shortages, need for investment in sewer infrastructure, and increased investment to reduce carbon dioxide emissions. Fortunately, there are examples around Asia of cities and nations tackling such issues head-on with surprising results. In Singapore, a city-sate with 4.5 million people squeezed onto just 270 square miles, conservation has long been an issue. According to Grace Fu, Singapore's senior minister of state for national development and education, Singapore had to constantly make a conscious trade-off between growth and environmental sustainability even during times of explosive economic expansion. As a result, half of Singapore is covered by green space today—proof that economic vibrancy and a livable, environmentally friendly city are not mutually exclusive.

The situation in New Delhi, by comparison, seems to be insurmountable with the squalor of immigrants who crowd this city of 16 million. Yet since 1999, New Delhi has been able to increase the green cover from less than three percent to nearly 30 percent of the city. All of the city's public transportation is run on compressed natural gas—with 100,000 public vehicles on the road, making the city the world leader. Still, 1,000 new owners of private vehicles hit the streets of New Delhi every day, so the government has started a comprehensive program to educate schoolchildren to reduce pollution and increase recycling.

Tadakatsu Sano, a partner and expert on international trade and government regulation for global law firm Jones Day, compares China's current challenges to Japan's in the 1960s and 1970s, saying China could learn from Japan's experience. For instance, Japan introduced laws to reduce pollution as early as 1967 (three years after the Tokyo Olympics and six years before the oil crisis). Japan was able to implement relevant policies in a methodical way, since the pollution crisis preceded the oil crisis. Sano feels that incentives and subsidies for environmentally friendly businesses are essential. He also suggests the implementation of public transportation systems such as those found in Tokyo and encourages a lower reliance on luxury cars.

In the fight for environmental sustainability, business leaders and entrepreneurs are often leading the way. For instance, Shi Zhengrong is CEO of Suntech, a company headquartered in China that leads the world in development of solar power technology. His business is built on both the environmental need for cleaner technology and the bottom-line pressure for energy alternatives as price of crude oil fluctuates wildly. New technology companies aren't the only ones leading the way—for Motorola, which has been a leader in the telecommunications industry since 1993, innovation is a driving force in all areas of the business. As a result, China is now Motorola's largest market and its biggest talent pool for new employees. Among its innovative practices, Motorola looks at ways to recycle parts and develop a market for used phones, rather than have them end in the landfill. Even businesses not associated with technology are embracing innovative technology to reduce impact on the environment. For example, PepsiCo Asia Pacific is reducing its water use by 20 percent by 2010.

Building the Future: Why High Fliers Are Getting Charitable

As the next generation of Asia Pacific business leaders look to carve a better future not only for themselves but for their communities, they are following in the footsteps of a growing number of today's senior executives, who turn their backs on the corporate world to move into nonprofit organizations. Hardly a day goes by without a multimillion-dollar salary being swapped for a more modest emolument. What's driving the sudden rush of altruism? The answer is partly an increasing demand by the nonprofit organizations themselves for better business practices in a sector traditionally driven more by values than the bottom line.

But the real reason behind the influx of top talent into the sector is that the wealthiest generation in history is now striding across the world stage, and our corporate leaders have the financial ability to do whatever they want. They've got everything, seen everything, been everywhere, and now they want to do some good without any financial constraints.

For example, when St. George Bank's chief financial officer, Steve McKerihan, felt the call to leave the bank and take the top finance job of the Anglican Church in Sydney, he gave up his US$1.5 million annual salary. Apart from his personal wealth, his shares in the bank after 22 years are worth about US$13.4 million and will provide him with an ongoing income stream.

Another former financial services executive is Michael Traill, the founding CEO of Social Ventures Australia, a new organization offering innovative solutions to entrenched community issues such as unemployment. During his 15 years with Macquarie Bank, Traill helped set up the private equity arm, growing a roughly US$41 million seed fund sevenfold over 10 years, with direct investments in more than 40 start-ups. Internet search pioneer and LookSmart founder Evan Thornley, who debuted on the BRW rich list with about US$475 million, left the company two years ago to join the board of the Brotherhood of St. Laurence in Melbourne. Thornley was a management consultant with McKinsey and is now using his skills in an organization whose aim is to alleviate poverty.

It's also cool to be charitable these days. Bill Gates is pouring billions into fighting AIDS in Africa, and U2's Bono has stepped onto the path pioneered by Sir Robert Geldof ("Sir Bob"), using his music to draw attention to the plight of the world's poor.

The sector is attracting increasing numbers of executives with strong financial management skills. The challenge for executives from the corporate world is that they may not have the patience to understand how nonprofits work. Corporate executives tend to move faster; they don't want to deal with the bureaucracies, and they want to see their accomplishment in faster terms than usually apply in nonprofits. In Australia, we have seen some examples of high performers who have not made it in the charities world due to their forceful style of management.

The successful charity leaders need to be both passionate about their mission and able to build consensus within the nonprofit's voluntary culture, where people are motivated by the cause itself, rather than by financial rewards.

They need to learn the art of being persuasive in seeking funds for their organizations, without coming across as typical corporate sales types. The complexities of the sector should not be underestimated by executives used to the more pragmatic world of business.

Don't Go Broke Not Making a Profit

Investment banker Paul Murnane was the founding chairman and is now a non-executive director of Multiple Sclerosis Limited. His skills in mergers and acquisitions came in handy when he helped merge the New South Wales and Victorian state societies of MS Australia. Murnane says the reason he chose to enter the sector was a belief that business should not be divorced from charities. "We all live in communities and I want to breathe healthy air just as much as the next business guy does," he says. "The dichotomy between the for-profit and nonprofits has always puzzled me because everyone goes home and they're in the community. To me, it just seems good business sense actually to be involved in the community because business operates with a license in effect by the community."

Murnane says that when he entered the sector, he found two contrasting attitudes—that of charities toward business, and business toward charities. "They had a 'business-is-evil, only-after-the-grubby-dollar, and untrustworthy' attitude and business generally had a view of nonprofits as being inefficient and focused on short-term projects rather than long-term strategies." He is impressed by the commitment of the staff in the nonprofit organizations. The danger for nonprofits focusing only on immediate projects is that they don't invest in capacity building for longer-term sustainability, he says. Murnane says that in charities, projects that have outlived their usefulness are often not canceled or reorganized, as they would be in the commercial world. "The tendency is to keep them afloat long beyond their use-by date," he says.

"They are passionate about the cause, and come to work each day with a focus and drive that can be lacking in the for-profit sector." Murnane says the challenge for a business leader is to come from the business world and shape a nonprofit organization so that it is more businesslike without becoming a business, "and without losing the passion and all the other things that motivate staff and volunteers."

Long-term success in nonprofits comes through quality leadership, Murnane says. "It comes down to the board appointing the right CEO, and holding the CEO and the leadership team responsible for producing a proper strategic plan, with proper processes to measure performance along the way.

"Strategic planning seems to be particularly weak in the nonprofit sector. It's not that great in the for-profit sector in many cases—but it seems particularly weak as most nonprofits struggle just to get through the year because a huge amount of time goes on fundraising."

Change Agents in Demand

Mark Lyons, adjunct professor of social economy at the University of Technology, Sydney, says performance measurement can be difficult in charities where there's no equivalent to a simple "return on funds invested" metric. He says there is a tendency to cut management costs to get funds to the frontline work of the organization. "That has frequently been a misguided approach."

Lyons says the excuse is often given that charities are too complex or too different for their work to be measured in a meaningful way—"but of course you can find metrics to measure their work," he says. "You can measure anything." He believes the sector is now attracting change agents sought out by boards that want to transform moribund organizations.

"Then new chief executives must be able to motivate the troops and tell a story that is both compelling and convincing. This is particularly true if you've come into an organization because the board wants you to change it. Many of our charities and many of the nonprofit organizations more broadly are seeing the need to dramatically review what they do and renew themselves, transform themselves."

Formerly in the stockbroking industry, Belinda Sullivan, CEO of the Eye Foundation, says she was drawn into the nonprofit sector by a desire to lead change—"and I think that is what is starting to attract other CEOs."

Sullivan says nonprofits are generally becoming more accountable, "and obviously the community is starting to drive that as well. There is definitely a shift to a much more commercial focus."

Charities must be sustainable, she says. She identifies two major issues:

- The need for a more commercial approach
- Fragmentation of the sector

"Everyone is looking at the bottom line and how much is actually taken up with administrative costs," she says. "Organizations may need to go through a transformational process and, possibly, be willing to take a one-off hit in order to improve efficiencies. Otherwise they will always be adopting a short-term approach and putting off crucial decisions."

Rationalization of the sector needs to be driven by governments and individuals, she says, adding that more than 50 eye health care organizations are in operation across Australia, each duplicating administration costs, and she points to the recent successful merger of several Royal Blind Societies into Vision Australia. The move cost US$4 million but was recouped in the first 12 months in operational savings.

Sullivan believes the future for the nonprofit sector lies in CEOs with a "commercial and performance mind-set" stepping in to run organizations more efficiently—"and ultimately providing a better impact for the community."

Efficiencies Spread the Money Further

Top charity leadership is a marriage of head and heart—the concern to make a difference combined with the ability to introduce new efficiencies and ideas. "When you are going out asking for money, you need to be as effective and efficient as possible with that dollar," says former Lumley General Insurance chief financial officer Mary-Anne Stephens. "To a large degree, nonprofits have done the best they could, but perhaps with the right skill sets and the right people they could do a bit better."

Stephens, now the COO of Children's Cancer Institute Australia, says the skills still needed in the sector include

- Broader operational experience
- Analytical and process improvement competencies
- Project management—"to reduce leakage and waste"
- Cash flow management expertise

"The sector needs to come out of itself and start actively going into the corporate sector and looking for people," Stephens says. "I wouldn't have thought twice about a nonprofit unless I had been approached. But now that I'm here I think, 'Wow, there's this whole world that's opened up and I can add a lot of value and feel good about what I'm doing.'"

Endnote

1 "Next Generation Leadership Survey," *Asia Society 2007 Asia 21 Young Leaders Summit Conference Report,* Heidrick & Struggles, February 2008. http://www.heidrick.com/NR/rdonlyres/D59CBE45-2BB8-4FF1-9662-DE3F94C4F8A5/0/HSAsia21reporty20Finalset080201.pdf

10

CONCLUSION

When company boards or executives examine their senior leadership in Asia Pacific, they really have only three basic questions to ask:

- What leadership do we need?
- What kind of leadership do we have today?
- How do we close the gap?

The answers to these questions are as varied as the companies, markets, and industries that operate here, in the fastest-growing business region in the world. This book, however, is a compendium of Heidrick & Struggles experience working with some of the greatest companies in the world on their answers to these questions. For an individual career, just insert the word *skills*—What leadership skills do I have? What leadership skills do I need? How do I close the gap?—and the same advice becomes a career guide toward the best practices of industry leaders in Asia Pacific.

In a nutshell, this is all Heidrick & Struggles does—speak to top managers and executive boards, and advise them on their leadership needs. While there is no magic formula for achieving success in Asia, the place to start is always analysis of the current situation, assessing the temperature of changing needs and looking for ways of bridging the distance between the two. Sometimes that's through addition of executives who bring needed experience with them; sometimes it's boosting the skills of existing staff to meet evolving challenges. Usually it's a combination of both.

Even during the explosive economic expansion of the region, anchored by the growing might of China and India, companies need senior managers at the top of their game to respond to the fast-moving changes in the business world—spotting new opportunities, responding to new challenges. As a result of the financial upheavals of 2008 and the contraction of the global economy, the need for great business leadership is now truly paramount. The opportunities for success and failure are even more razor-edge, especially in the dynamic environment that is Asia.

Companies and executives who emerge from adversity are always strengthened by the experience, and their standing in the market is solidified. During the fast-paced and difficult decisions that tough times require, those who eventually succeed never forget one important point—their human capital, the people who work with them, is their most important resource. That point is easy to forget in a tough economy, especially when impartial decisions regarding staffing levels and needs often result in reduction. But that only underlines the importance of knowing the human capital in-house and in the marketplace to best work the decks and steer the ship through troubled waters. How well the people at all levels are managed and deployed will determine which companies and executives succeed, and which fail.

Here is a review of the main points made in this book:

Chapter 1: The Rise and Rise of Asia Pacific

The cities of Shenzhen in China and Bangalore in India represent the new poles of the growing power of Asia in the business world. The brains of Bangalore and the manufacturing brawn of Shenzhen are the twin axes of the burgeoning development happening in economies around the region. They are the leading edge of the second wave of Asia's impact on the global business world, following the first, which was led half a century ago by postwar Japan.

Asian business is coming of age at a time when technology and globalization are rewriting the rules for 21st-century business. Both have opened rich new veins of products to sell and places to sell them. The playing field has been leveled across borders and powerful new corporate players are emerging in Asia.

Asia Pacific Companies Go Global

As domestic companies in Asia expand their global reach, challenges emerge. Here are the key steps companies take when broadening operations across Asian borders:

- Establish a beachhead. As companies establish their initial offshore presence in the host nation, they ship executives from the home country to learn the vagaries of the new market.
- Face the challenge of cultural differences. Differences in national culture are evaluated and efforts are made to address them.
- Find local talent for local operations. Executives are brought on board from the host country as the company expands beyond the exploratory phase. Then the trick is to retain the smartest executives, the ones who learn quickly from the newcomer and thus increase their market value.
- Export the corporate culture. The corporate culture is just as important to the company's long-term success as the culture in which the operation is now immersed, so the company makes an effort to instill the values into the new host nation executives.
- Develop global leaders. There is a pressing need for executives from both home and target countries to be given "global" experience in order to enhance the organization's flexibility and competitiveness.

The Answer

Chief executives in the Asia Pacific are already experiencing leadership pressures and are taking steps to lead robust talent management strategies such as these:

- Exposing executives to deeper levels of strategy making and business planning to create development opportunities for them.
- Recognizing that people's long-term career and life aspirations are inextricably linked and moving to assist where possible.
- Rewarding top talent in more creative ways. For example, some banks are offering executives the choice of 75 percent of full pay for a yearlong leave after four years on the job to pursue other interests (write a book, start a business).
- Developing the management team to appreciate and respond to the emerging demands of leadership across the five generations that will be simultaneously employed by organizations to meet their needs over the next 10 years.

Chapter 2: The Evolving C-Suite

A successful CEO succession plan is a four-step process, driven by the board and supported by external professionals:

1. Inclusive analysis and planning, bringing together all key stakeholders from board members to investors.
2. Internal and external candidate identification and preparation, with all candidates compared on the same basis.
3. Decision phase, with transparency and full communication with stakeholders, shareholders, and board. Like the photo finish in a tight horse race, this transparency can reveal in close-up what might not be obvious from a distance.
4. Transition to the CEO suite, with advisory coaching and sustained "on-boarding" to ensure the executive is comfortable with any new aspects of the game.

Chief Operating Officer

Broadly speaking, it is possible to describe the role of the COO as a *head-down* position, focused on the operational details and day-to-day execution necessary for success, while the CEO is a *head-up* role looking outward with a strategic view to make sure the business does not miss changes in the industry and technology.

Three major styles of COO:

- *Mentor:* Helps accelerate the CEO's own development as leader at a time when the growth of the company is threatening to get ahead of the CEO's managerial experience.
- *Change agent:* Helps turn around the company's troubled areas, as when a technology company is having trouble with sales and marketing.
- *Partner:* Often called "two in a box," this type of COO role requires an executive willing to forsake the ambition to become CEO. This approach works especially well in family companies.

Chief Financial Officer

The chief financial officer's role has changed considerably since the days when the incumbent may have been regarded simply as a number-cruncher. Today's CFO must have a symbiotic relationship with the CEO, to turn strategic vision into reality.

Key attributes:

- Financial understanding of the company's activities
- Ability to clearly communicate the business outcomes
- Ability to explain the operations of the business and its progress
- Awareness and appreciation of key drivers and risks

Chief Human Resources Officer

The field of human resources has changed dramatically. Formerly focused on process and administration, the chief human resources officer is now focused on behavioral science and ways to get organizations and individuals to behave in different and more effective ways. US and European companies are coming to grips with the new role of CHRO, but Asian companies are lagging far behind in appreciating how HR has changed and how strategic the CHRO has become.

Chief Marketing Officer

A new generation of marketing leaders has emerged. Guiding more than just the classic marketing mix, successful chief marketing officers are driving corporate strategy, holding general management responsibility, and developing next-generation talent in a function that was once relegated to the "four P's" of marketing (product, price, place, and promotion). As the CMO role redefines itself across the business landscape, marketing leaders struggle to overcome functional stereotypes and prove their value to the organization.

Chief Risk Officer

The role of chief risk officer has evolved—once the preserve of the major financial institutions, it has increasingly been adopted by a wide range of industries.

The CRO role is splitting into two distinct positions:

- The CRO as a genuine partner in business management, playing a critical role in growth strategy, product strategy, and mergers and acquisitions.

- The "chief compliance officer," shouldering the responsibility for corporate-level reporting, operational risk, and regulatory compliance. Regulations such as Sarbanes-Oxley, Basel II and a plethora of other standards have raised the workload to the point that a new senior position is necessary.

Chief Information Officer

Emerging from the high-tech world, CIOs are now charged with leading cultural change to enable reengineering of business processes across the enterprise. The future generation of CIOs will take on greater responsibility for the profitability of their business, as well as the creation of analytical models to understand the behavior of customers.

Key attributes:

- Credibility with the CEO
- Superior communication skills
- Ability to look right across the business and into the future

Chief Procurement Officer

Chief procurement officers coordinate the global purchasing of commodities and the development of standardized contracts for items ranging from travel to heavy equipment. This powerful position first appeared in the United States, migrated to Europe, and will be seen increasingly in Asia, as more companies move their CPOs to the region.

Not typically considered the heroes of their business, they find their prestige within an organization rises in tandem with cost pressures and the need to streamline costs.

Chief Privacy Officer

The CPO is also a position that is rising in importance as collection of data becomes more important, and safeguarding of that information more subject to privacy laws and litigation. CPOS need the ability to draw on a broad range of fields, such as legal, government affairs, technology, auditing, and business intelligence.

Private Equity Executive

Many executives in Asia are leaving careers at multinational companies to join the burgeoning ranks of private equity companies looking to invest in the region. However, the role is very different from its equivalent at multinational companies—private equity firms must look at a broad range of investment opportunities, not those limited by an executive's own industry experience.

Communications between strategic PE investors and management is also far more transparent. In a public company with numerous stakeholders and prerequisite disclosure protocols, communications tend to be more guarded.

Chapter 3: Getting to the Top: Leadership Development

Before trying for the corner office, make sure you really want it. The sacrifices and hard work required aren't for everyone. Top executives must have or nurture:

- Total commitment to the role—you have to want it, and you have to be married to it (to put it first in your life)
- Communication skills—particularly listening, influencing and negotiating
- Congeniality—the ability to build relationships with people you might otherwise detest
- Consultative character—allowing others to help you solve problems

Three main qualities that enable a C-level executive to be successful:

- The quality of the people the executive appoints to surrounding positions
- The quality of those the executive chooses to work with
- The quality of the decision making that follows

Two critical capabilities:

- The ability to get along with people. This is not just about being liked and loved; it is about being able to understand people and to discern what drives them, and being able to influence them in a collaborative way.
- The ability to get things done. People should notice that something happens when you are there that would not happen if you weren't.

Breaking Through to Senior Management

Technical skills may move someone from the bottom to middle level ranks, but what sets senior executives above the rest is "soft skills"—the ability to manage interrelationships with a variety of different types of people, and to motivate them toward results.

Cultural Awareness Is Key

Aside from people skills, understanding a company's culture is key for breaking through to senior management. Those who move from company to company throughout their career will need to be acutely sensitive to the nuances of a new employer—even companies in the same industry can have radically different cultures. Trust and confidence must be nurtured with home office as well as around the region.

What Makes a Leader in a Flat World?

When searching for new leaders in an increasingly flat world, these are some of the key questions in evaluating candidates:

- How does this person go about building a team?
- Was this person effective—how, specifically?
- What results were achieved?
- What is this person's management style?

Commitment to Asia

Key things when considering moving to a career in Asia:

- Asia is no longer a corporate backwater; the executive talent in the region rivals that found in developed markets.
- Expat packages are increasingly uncommon; many Westerners with careers in the region are now on local packages.
- To land a role, it is key to demonstrate a firm commitment to a long-term career in the region.
- It is best to knock on company doors directly; executive search firms focus on the needs of their clients, who seek executives with experience in the region.

Are Your Executives On Board or Overboard?

Unsuccessful placement of top executives can cost millions of dollars and destabilize the firm. Some key reasons why new executives fall:

- Failing to build relationships with the board
- Bringing in new team members who do not understand the business
- Not consulting widely enough, and not sharing the results of consultation with those who could help execute a turnaround plan

The on-boarding process in bringing a new executive into the company fold must be pervasive and ongoing. Here are nine steps for successful on-boarding:

1. Start on-boarding during recruitment, ensuring a staged schedule of contacts between the candidate and the company.
2. Designate an appropriate mentor who will help the newcomer build a strong network within the senior levels.
3. Show the incoming executive exactly how to get things done in the new environment.
4. Tailor the on-boarding program to the individual, taking into account the newcomer's strengths and weaknesses and areas that will need critical support in the coming months.
5. Define deliverables covering the first 60 and 120 days, the first six months and first year, so the executive can drive revenue while assimilating the new culture.
6. Get the executive on a project team—any team. The fastest way to get a new executive moving is by total immersion.
7. Integrate the executive into the peer group, seeking out those with mutual interests as well as recent arrivals.
8. Provide regular, constructive feedback.
9. Intervene early and often. Timely corrective action is important. Take a 360-degree "pulse check" with the new executive, the team, and peers to work out what is going well and what is not. Discuss ways to remove roadblocks and adjust resources to encourage success and prevent derailment. Convey successes widely and communicate a company-wide "buzz" around the achievements of the new executive.

Chapter 4: Building and Keeping Teams

Human resources departments of multinational corporations are trying to establish or enlarge their presence in Asia. The staggering growth and further potential of the region cannot escape the notice of any company with a global vision. Given this situation, the demand for qualified, talented and effective executives has outpaced the supply.

Succession Strategies

As boards grapple with CEO succession strategies, senior executives must cultivate future company leaders within their ranks and without. Effective succession planning requires at least five steps:

1. Identify future leaders.
2. Assess the talent against current and emerging needs.
3. Address their development needs by training, job rotation, or mentoring and coaching.
4. Monitor candidate progress.
5. Constantly benchmark candidates against potential external hires.

Internal Versus External Hiring

The question of whether to hire from within or outside an organization has no single correct answer, but clever companies answer yes to both. They promote from within when possible, provided their internal talent is first rate, and from outside when they realize their internal resources fail to stack up to external benchmarks. For example, a pharmaceutical company with marketing challenges can look to industries such as consumer products, which have a low profit margin and emphasize marketing for volume sales.

The Candidate Is King

The prevailing attitude in many Asian markets is that companies choose their people. In today's competitive landscape, however, it is not companies choosing the best people but the best people choosing companies. The global war for talent is over, and talent has won: talent has plenty of opportunities to choose from throughout the region and around the world. As a result, competitive compensation and perks, as well as a focus on career path advantages, are increasingly becoming important tools for Asian companies to retain employees with high potential.

Interim Options

Sometimes, the best person for the job is a temporary one. An effective part-time staff strategy is crucial even in upper and senior management.

Interim executives fall into three main categories:

- Interim executives brought in for a fixed term
- Interim-to-permanent executives
- Project executives brought in for pre- to post-implementation

Companies are moving toward a flexible workforce to best address stakeholder needs with this blend of factors:

- Permanent employees with access to full-time, part-time, and flexible work practices, such as some days working from home
- Contractors hired for specific assignments
- Short-term interim professionals, as well as more generic skills

Chapter 5: Executive Talent Management

For companies hiring a leader in Asia, it is important to have a comprehensive on-boarding strategy in place, which should involve the new executive from Asia spending time in the head office, becoming familiar with the company and forming relationships with new colleagues. Tailoring corporate culture to a local market can be challenging, but it is essential for success. While corporate practices must be tailored to local staff and conditions, "going native"—that is, disconnecting from headquarters—can be a quick path out the door.

New Challenges in a Virtual World

For executives in the new, disembodied organizations, these are the keys to communication:

- Connections—maintaining contact both at a distance and with regular "face time."

- Relationships—building trust through open communications, be it phone, e-mail, or in person
- Common context—understanding the context in which colleagues work, wherever they are, as well as the common aims and goals of the organization

Winning Trust, Driving Success

Important points toward building trust:

- Obtain a detailed understanding of your role's scope from senior management.
- Show an interest in team activities such as meetings, and follow up on team action plans.
- Win over key influencers in the team.
- If possible, have your remuneration tied to the performance of the team.

Dealing with Prima Donnas

Best game plan for dealing with prima donnas:

- Remember that aggressive behavior can be a source of self-esteem for prima donnas; leaders need to find other ways to fuel this self-esteem.
- Act as soon as prima donna behavior becomes apparent—avoid procrastination.
- When speaking with a prima donna, offer specific examples of the behavior that needs to change—avoid making it an issue of general personality.
- Stress how a change in behavior will help benefit the individual over the long run.
- Avoid favoritism: in today's team-centric world, favoritism can be dangerous for morale.

Fighting Office Warfare

Key tips for resolving office conflicts:

- Act quickly when the signs of a conflict emerge.
- Sit down with the warring parties and outline why it is in their long-term interest to resolve their differences.

- Listen as they outline their grievances.
- Have each party summarize the other's point of view, encouraging them to note points of common ground.
- Encourage both sides to make some face-saving concessions, and get agreement on the steps both parties need to take to resolve the conflict.

Managing a Multi-Generational Workforce

Executives managing a multi-generational workforce are reporting that younger workers may be more motivated by challenge than by money. Conversely, they've found that older workers often want more pay—reflecting their experience—and are less comfortable with strict performance-based compensation.

There are four things leaders can do to better manage multiple generations:

- Ensure open communication. Honestly address concerns. Being open and transparent will go a long way toward bringing issues into the open and retaining your best people.
- Respect the different values held by different age groups. This simply means being aware of the lack of loyalty of young people—and the possibly excessive loyalty of older people.
- Encourage intergenerational partnerships and collaboration. You need to teach the older workers to listen for the fresh ideas of the younger generation, and teach younger leaders to seek out and value the experience of the older people.
- Remain flexible. You have to be flexible for the fickle younger generation, but also look for ways to retain the knowledge—if not the days of work—of more experienced executives. They hold a lot of your corporate memory, which is better with you than with a competitor.

Chapter 6: Mentoring, Coaching and Setting an Example

Make Yourself a Mentor, Coach

Coaching and *mentoring* are often used interchangeably, but there are distinct differences between them:

MENTORS

- Share their own experience to help bridge the learning gap of the employee.
- Use interpersonal skills to connect their experience in a context that the employee understands and can apply to the current situation.
- Champion their charges—advocate for them within the company, pushing them into projects and assignments that help round out their skills.

COACHES

- Help employees help themselves—coaches don't teach from their experience, they help people make sense of their own experience.
- Use and help the employee develop intrapersonal skills—knowing yourself and asking yourself the right questions to make the right decisions.
- Employ a Socratic method, simply listening and asking the right questions.

The Gentle Art of Coaching

Tips on successful coaching:

- Remember that coaching is guiding, not telling or doing.
- Before a coaching session, whether planned or not, pause to decide on the key objectives you would like the session to achieve.
- Ask the right questions—and avoid questions that may put an employee on the defensive.
- Listen carefully to the answers to your questions, and offer your viewpoint only where it will be helpful to move the employee forward.

Dealing with an Underperformer

Steps for dealing with an underperformer:

- Be proactive: arrange a meeting to discuss the issue.
- Make sure the employee knows you are both on the same side.

- Agree on what the issue is—and the steps to change things.
- Write down the agreed action plan.
- Schedule subsequent meetings to review progress.

New Blood, New Values

Seven fundamental skills to become an effective change agent in your organization:

- Make your case for change.
- Have a clear vision.
- Develop a strategy.
- Work out how much organizational capacity there is to enact the change.
- Introduce strong motivation for change to the business.
- Communicate effectively: "Keep on top of the messages that are being transmitted through the organization."
- Be consistent in your own behavior: "Model the change that you are trying to make."

Transformation—Fast or Slow?

Four things to remember to become an effective change manager:

- Stick to your principles and focus on what changes are needed.
- Resist the temptation to get sucked back into making incremental rather than major change.
- Be resilient.
- Look for small successes and reward examples of excellence where you find it.

Starting Off Strong

Here are the ways new executives add value early on:

- Spend informal time with team members, getting to know their role and coaching them.
- Get to know junior people, perhaps suggesting new roles or responsibilities to help them add depth to their careers.

- Spend time following up with people, helping them achieve their objectives.
- Celebrate achievements, both major and minor.

Courage is not about being fearless. Nor is it about being the toughest. It is about acting in spite of fear. Moral courage. Employees and their managers need calm, focus, clarity, personal courage and real leadership.

Communicate; Create Clarity

The worst fear is nothing more than the unknown. Be honest with your people. Tell them what you do and don't know. Ask them for what they know. When you don't have anything to tell them, then tell them that. Listen to those who need to communicate with you. Focus on what is important to them, not you.

Make Imperfect Decisions

There is no time, need, nor room now for the irrational quest for perfection that creates stalled momentum. Plan to make imperfect decisions to ensure that the factor of time is appropriately considered. Ensure momentum. Break inertia.

Be Present; Be Seen

Though you yourself may be angry, depressed and confused, this is not the time to show such feelings. This is a time to get out among your people as much as you can. Answer their questions. Be seen to be approachable. People are looking for evidence to be alarmed. Don't let your distance or your countenance provide that evidence.

Don't Criticize

This is not the time to berate anyone for recent past mistakes or dwell on the myriad internal excuses that will be rising in you for "how we got into this mess." Keep your mind clearly focused on the future for your people. Offer them the opportunity to clean up for themselves. Forgive those who falter initially. They are probably doing the best they can.

Manage Yourself; Set the Example and Find Examples

Manage anxiety. Believe in yourself. Focus on the higher intent of the organization rather than the last dollar saved. Smile. Make time for people. Be made of Teflon. Seek feedback. Be available. Be personal.

Learn, Unlearn, Relearn

Make sure you are informed. Be a source of external knowledge and cling to the data that drives evidence for optimism. Reach out to other CEOs, sources of confidants and discreet support beyond your organization. Find someone you can share your concerns with who will not judge you and who will benefit in return.

Chapter 7: Enter the Dragon: China

A survey of leaders in China showed that almost all deemed the ability to attract, develop and retain leadership teams their number one challenge. CEOs and HR executives here have battled this issue on three distinct fronts:

- China's unique emerging market model
- The huge influence of multinational companies entering the market
- Increasingly aggressive local companies

More than in most markets, companies in China need to spend time and resources to identify and retain staff. For example, the GE-Jack Welch model of identifying the top 20 percent and the "vital 70 percent" in the middle, and annually shedding the bottom 10 percent, won't work in China. Instead, this model should be followed:

- Lead category: top five percent of employees.
- Sustain category: the next 20 percent of vital employees.
- Potential group: the middle 50 percent of employees earmarked for development.
- Gray community: the lower 20 percent, who should be evaluated for fit.
- Remove: the lowest five percent of employees.

More time must be spent on evaluation and development because of the fast-moving nature of the market and the enormous natural turnover as employees "job hop" from one opportunity to the next.

Winning China's War for Talent

In China, many hiring practices are reactive, and companies set out to hire only when a gap appears in their management team. Little thought is given to a candidate's strategic fit in the organization. Hiring in China can also be ad hoc, with no structured recruiting process in place.

The first step HR departments can take is to set up a clear recruitment process. The process needs to lead all the way from the headcount plan and job description through the new hire's first year on the job.

The job market in China is extremely fast-paced: quality candidates often have a range of career opportunities, and may lack the patience to wait for a company that is dragging its feet. Leadership also needs to be prepared to sign off quickly on new candidates.

Many companies are entering China hoping for a low-cost market, but have found that the limited pool of quality candidates means that costs in China's labor market are inflated. Candidates typically have a good sense of their market value and companies must be willing to pay the price to get the right candidates.

Managing China's Industrial Growth

The outlook for China's industrial category remains strong, with many pundits saying that China will continue to enjoy five to eight percent GDP growth rates annually over the next 10 to 20 years. The slowdown in the United States and Europe could further add to industrial growth as hold-outs to outsourcing find few alternatives.

There has been an evolution in Chinese industrial growth, drawing senior managers at first from abroad, then from the large pool of Chinese expatriates. Now the trend is shifting toward local Chinese talent to lead operations.

Key elements to attracting the right leaders to harness China's industrial might:

- Developing a culture of building and retaining winning teams
- Fostering top-down ownership of leadership development
- Integrating multiple stakeholders (both internal and external)

- Redefining the role of HR as an asset manager and the key custodian of a company's culture of building winning teams
- Investing in technology and inserting alternative culturally attuned assessment methodologies into the corporate DNA
- Ensuring technology and assessment become core systems for the company—no point having superior senior managers if the rest of the organization cannot support their initiatives or is out of synch culturally with the management elite
- Developing innovative risk management strategies and processes for management development

The Cure for High Turnover in China

Keeping the current team happy is not just a matter of offering more money; it requires focusing on career development. Talent must be identified and reviewed on a regular basis, and comprehensive talent development plans must be in place. Training programs are essential.

The right compensation is, of course, essential. Only the very strongest companies can afford to compensate top talents at or below market levels. All others have little choice but to pay above market, particularly to attract top talents. To create incentives to stay, companies are increasing the variable rate of pay packages in the form of performance bonuses, and they are issuing stock options and restricted stock units that often vest years later. They offer cars with drivers, housing subsidies, executive MBA sponsorships and savings plans.

Battlefield Promotions

In China, many executives are flying up the ranks and crossing from one industry to another. The phenomenon mainly exists in the key coastal cities where multinationals have their primary focus: Shanghai, Beijing, and Guangzhou. It is also starting to appear in key regional cities such as Dalian, Chengdu, and Wuhan.

Executives who have risen too fast simply may not have the experience to lead large teams in a challenging market, thus jeopardizing their career and their company's bottom line. What's more, such promotions can stoke internal rivalries: if one executive gets promoted, others will notice and begin looking for their own promotion.

Long-Term Career Paths

Overpromotion is not guaranteed to improve retention—at best, it is a quick fix to placate the ambitions of a top talent. Instead, companies should have clear long-term career paths for their top talent—often, such individuals depart because a career path has not been made clear to them.

One well-tested way to help top talent develop is to rotate executives through headquarters for an extended period, six months to a few years. Such rotations should not be done merely for the sake of doing so, but should offer meaningful work experience, preferably in a new, challenging area that broadens an executive's career horizons.

Chapter 8: The Elephant in the Room: India

For years, companies have been using India as an outsourcing center. But with the fast-growing domestic market, many domestic companies are now bringing in expatriate senior executives to help tap the growing business potential here, as well as fill in gaps for senior managers with international experience.

Meanwhile, multinational firms are moving more top executives and offices to India to be at the center of the rapidly expanding market.

Value Proposition Versus China

Compared to China, Indian employees are gaining advantage with a higher percentage of the population aged 25 to 34 years old with a college education, as well as strong English skills. But challenges remain. The key problem faced by Indian managers in achieving global leadership positions is lack of exposure to global scale and best practices. Indian corporations have been inward looking and protected. Many are only now beginning to compete in the global marketplace.

Next Outsourcing Wave: Moving Up Value Chain

Although Indian business has exploded with low-cost centers for back-office processing and software development, the situation is changing fast. Beyond short-term cost savings, multinational companies are making medium and long-term investments toward developing India's deep talent pool into higher-value areas such as research and development, financial information, and senior corporate management.

Domestic Market Explodes

Besides its outsourcing prowess, India is making great strides as a market in its own right. Take for example India's retail sector—which is predicted to grow by 40 percent annually until 2011, when it should be worth more than US$400 billion.

In this cauldron of activity, India's retailers need to avoid having their fingers burned. Disproportionately high real estate prices, poorly connected distribution networks, and a lack of modern supply chain logistics and skilled personnel, as well as an elementary regulatory system, are all potential hazards. As a result, India's local retail players have yet to close the gap in efficiency when measured against global operational metrics.

Growing Pains for Professional Service Firms

Professional service firms such as management consulting organizations are in a tough fight to attract both top talent and clients. Regardless of the various challenges that India's PSFs face, they will have to orchestrate well-tuned recruitment and retention strategies and to practice what they preach, so to speak. Keep the following principles in mind:

- *Be your firm's investment manager:* Invest resources in building a long-term strategy, and don't just punt on short-term efforts to capture growth.
- *Be your firm's management consultant:* Carefully plan all the different aspects of the firm's growth strategy in relation to its talent needs.
- *Be your firm's public relations executive:* Communicate and rally enthusiasm for the firm's vision.

On the Migration Path Home

More and more Indians whose families have moved abroad are moving back to India for growing opportunities back home. With their international experience, these people are quickly being snapped up.

This new breed of "R2I" (return to India) employees can be broadly broken down into these classes:

- *Fast trackers:* Executives who started their careers in India before being promoted to regional roles outside India or to more senior roles in other countries.
- *Transferees:* Executives already working in India on expatriate packages, having been transferred or seconded to their employer's Indian subsidiary or joint venture on short-term contracts lasting three to five years, or on permanent contracts.
- *Emerging managers:* Professionals in their mid-20s or early 30s who come armed with prestigious academic qualifications from the United States or Europe.
- *Domain experts:* Indians with an international track record in industries that are now expanding at home, such as real estate, clean-tech investing, and finance.
- *Relationship networkers:* A relatively small group, relationship networkers cover the Indian market from overseas, such as a private banker covering the Indian market from Singapore, Hong Kong, or Dubai.

Chapter 9: The Future of Business Leadership in Asia Pacific

Looking at the decades to come, we expect to see dramatic changes in the way business is done in Asia Pacific. For example, the next wave of exports from China will be senior executives. In addition, business in the region will grow both greener and more involved in charitable work.

Executives: The Next Wave of Chinese Exports

By 2030, when many economists predict China will have eclipsed the United States as the world's top market, multinationals will be scouring China to find leadership not only in the Chinese market but in markets in developed countries to offset the Baby Boomer depletion of senior executives worldwide.

Top Chinese executives in 2030 will have a different mind-set from their fathers', looking at lifestyle issues and advantages offered by positions abroad. In a dramatic role reversal, companies in developed markets will offer expat packages to help woo Chinese executives to locate overseas.

Innovation and Asia's Future Business Leaders

Company leaders are finding innovative ways to achieve the goals of growing market share, reducing costs, and increasing a company's standing as a responsible corporate player in the communities.

Rapid economic growth without proper regulatory controls has caused severe environmental problems in Asia, particularly in China and India. While Western industrial centers went through a similar phase when they were first developing, China and India are under increased scrutiny because of their sheer size and emergence at a time where greenhouse gas emissions are a global concern.

As a result, many company leaders and entrepreneurs in Asia are leading the way to develop innovative methods to promote sustainability while building the bottom line.

Building the Future: Why High Flyers Are Getting Charitable

As the next generation of Asia Pacific business leaders look to carve a better future not only for themselves but also for their communities, they are following in the footsteps of a growing number of today's senior executives who have turned their backs on the corporate world to move into nonprofit organizations. What's driving the sudden rush of altruism? The answer is partly an increasing demand by the not-for-profit organizations themselves for better business practices in a sector traditionally driven more by values than the bottom line. But also financially successful executives are looking for greater fulfillment in life—to add value and feel good about their work.

INDEX

A
ABB, 124
Accenture, 85, 106, 143
Adams, Kirby, 18
Adidas, 132
Aditya Birla Hypermarkets, 141
Aditya Birla Retail, 141
Advertising Age, 39
Alcatel, 133
Allaby, Mark, 85
Arthur Andersen, 142
Ambit Corporate Finance, 143
AMD, 143, 144
American Express, 108, 133
American Express Bank, 133
AMP, 64, 70
Anglican Church, 159
Ansett, 52
ANZ, 52
AOL India, 133
Ardi, Dana, 88
Argy Philip, 47
Asia Pacific, 1, 2, 4, 5, 13, 15–19, 24, 27, 28, 48, 59, 61, 69, 73, 74, 93–95, 106, 119, 125, 147, 151, 155, 159, 165–167, 186, 187
Asia Society, 155, 156, 163
Asian Institute of Management, 60
AT&T, 108
Australian Red Cross Blood Service, 80
Autodesk, 144

B
Baby Boomer, 15, 17, 76, 92, 151, 153, 186
Back-end, 140
Ballmer, Steve, 32
Bangalore, 13, 14, 134, 138, 139, 144, 166
Bank of America, 86
Barlett, Christopher, 18
Barnett Lee, 64
Barry, Lisa, 106
Basel II, 40, 170
Bashinsky, Alec, 63
Baxter Laboratories, 18
Bayman, Scott, 144

Becton, Dickinson, and Company, 56
Beel, Wayne, 78
Beijing, 26, 119, 128, 130, 152, 157, 183
Belgacom, 105
BellSouth, 108
Bennett, Nathan, 32, 33
Berlin Wall, 13, 147
Berman, Russell, 141
Bharti Airtel, 133
Bharti Enterprises, 135
Bharti, Mittal Sunil, 135
Bharti Televentures, 144
BHP Billiton, 16, 20, 22, 23, 27, 52, 80
Big Bazaar, 140
Bill, Brown, 77
Biocon, 139
Birla Group, 141
Biyani Kishore, 140
Blackstone, 47
Blue-chip, 25
BlueScope, 18, 21, 24, 25, 30, 41
Board Governance, 25, 64, 69, 155
Board of Directors, 136
Boardrooms, 5, 38, 83
Boeing, 134, 135
Bono, 160
Borghesi, Carol, 133
Boston Consulting Group, 43, 142
Bottom-line, 158
Bradley, Paul W., 61
Brambles, 30, 105
Branson, Richard, 56
Brin, Sergey, 33
British Telecom (BT), 33
Brotherhood of St. Laurence, 159
BRW, 159
Buffet, Warren, 3
Bull, Trevor, 133
Business Process Outsourcing (BPO), 135, 138
Bygodt, Loic, 135

C
Cantonese, 24
CapGemini, 144
Carrefour, 140

189

INDEX

Carter, Holt Harvey, 80
Carlyle Group, 48, 49
Cass Business School, 154
Cata, Carlos, 39
Cathay Pacific Airways, 53
CCMP Capital Asia, 48
Celestica, 102
Cement Australia, 77, 78
"Chainsaw" Al Dunlap, 33
Chambers, John, 143
Chan, Ambrose, 22
Chaney, Michael, 30, 31
Chang, Herman, 48
Chenault, Kenneth, 108
Chengdu, 130, 183
Chennai, 133, 139, 144
Chernin, Peter, 32
Chicago School of Business, 60
Chief Executive, 5, 16, 20, 28, 30, 32, 41, 62, 78, 161, 167
Chief Executive Officer (CEO), 2, 5–8, 16–24, 27, 29–35, 38, 40, 43, 46, 48, 51, 55, 56, 61–64, 70, 72, 76, 78, 82, 86–90, 97, 99, 102, 103, 105, 108, 112, 117–119, 126–128, 130, 133–135, 141, 143, 144, 154, 158, 159, 161, 162, 168, 169, 170, 174, 181
Chief Financial Officer (CFO), 8, 33–35, 38, 40, 41, 51, 77, 133, 159, 162, 168, 169
Chief Human Resources Officer (CHRO), 8, 35–38, 169
Chief Information Officer (CIO), 42–44, 51–54, 64, 70, 71, 105–108, 170
Chief Marketing Officers (CMO), 8, 38, 39, 144, 169
Chief Operating Officer (COO), 8, 32, 33, 40, 48, 77, 132, 163, 168
Chief Procurement Officers (CPO), 44, 45, 170
Chief Risk Officer (CRO), 40–42, 169
Child care, 93
Children's Cancer Institute Australia, 163
China, 1, 2, 5–8, 10, 14–16, 18, 19, 22, 24–26, 45, 47, 48, 83, 95, 117–133, 136, 137, 147–154, 156–158, 165, 166, 181–184, 186, 187
China (PRC), 117, 118, 120, 121, 124, 182
Chisholm, Sam, 76, 77
Chow, Freddie, 129
Chrismer, Bob, 64
Chua, Chris, 55, 57
Chung Cheng Yeo, 107
Cisco, 134, 137, 143, 144
Cisco Intel Alliance, 143
Cisco Systems, 137, 143
Citibank, 135
Citicorp, 139
Citigroup, 44
C-level, 4, 46, 51, 53, 54, 63, 78, 97, 171
Cliché, 32
Close-up, 31, 168
Coca-Cola, 39, 48
Co-chairman, 18
Cochlear, 16, 24, 26, 27, 80
Co-founder, 18
Cohade, Pierre, 74
Cold War, 13
Coleman, Vicki, 71

Coles Myer, 52, 53–54, 105
Collins, Jim, 10
Command-and-control, 92
Communist Party, 153
Company-wide, 65, 173
Concours Group, 93
Consumer, 22, 24, 25, 28, 39, 46, 59, 73, 130, 131, 140, 174
Coomer, Michael, 43, 53
Counterproductive, 91, 108
Craig, Barrett, 143
Credit Lyonnais, 17
Cross-border, 20
Cross-cultural, 8, 127, 142
Curtis, Karen, 46
Customer-focused, 105

D

Dalian, 130, 183
Danny Dale, 43, 44
Davies, Andrew, 133
Decision-making, 23, 53, 145, 171
Delhi, 144
Dell, 19, 33, 56
Dell Computer, 33
Dell, Michael, 33
Deloitte Touche Tohmatsu, 63, 106, 157
Delong, Thomas J., 141
Delphi, 48
Denby, Andrew, 141
Deng, James, 128
Deng Xiaoping, 14, 153
Deutsche Bank, 135
DHL Express Asia Pacific, 73
Diaspora, 148–149
Diversity, 4, 39, 83, 106
Dot-com, 44
Dr. Reddy's Labs, 138
Dramis, Fran, 108
Dunlap, Al, 33
Dychtwald, Ken 93
Détente, 13

E

Economist Intelligence Unit (EIU), 150
Economist, 17, 153
EDS, 93
Education, 16, 55, 137, 150, 153, 154, 158, 184
Edwards, David N., 61
Elfrink, William, 134
Ellison, Larry, 33
E-mail, 43, 58, 75, 85, 90, 103, 176
Emmanuel, Jeff, 34
Emotional Intelligence (EQ), 3, 4, 27, 118
Enterprise, 25, 34, 41, 42, 44, 106, 117, 130, 134, 135
Entwistle, Brooks, 133
Erickson, 93
Erickson, Tamara, 93
Ernst & Young, 138
Ethnocentricity, 28
Evil Empire, 13
Executive Assessment, 119
Executive Recruiting, 5, 62

F

Executive Search, 58, 61, 172
Eye Foundation, 162

F

Fairfax, 93
Farrell, Diana, 118, 149
FedEx Corporation, 88, 109
Ferrier, Andrew, 20, 24
Financial services, 34, 42, 43, 70, 77, 79, 85, 139, 144, 159
Financial Times, 150
Fiorina, Carly, 6
Fletcher, John, 105
Fonterra, 16, 20, 24
Food and Drug Administration (FDA), 138
FoodWorld, 140
Fortune, 14, 152
Foster, George, 19, 20
Foster, Warwick, 70, 71
Fox Network, 32
Freescale, 45
Friel, Tom, 72
Fu, Grace, 158
Fudan University of Shanghai, 150
Fundraising, 161
Future Group, 140

G

Garg, Mohanty Soma, 73
Gates, Bill, 160
GE Capital, 40
GE Plastics, 138
Geldof, Robert, 160
General Electric (GE), 3, 7, 40, 118, 120, 124, 138, 144, 181
Generation X, 92, 153
Generation Y, 93–95, 152
Georgia Institute of Technology, 32
GE-Welch, 120, 181
Giants, 45, 140, 151
Globe-hopping, 19
Globe-trotting, 150
Goldman Sachs (India) Securities, 133
Goodyear Chip, 16, 20, 22, 27
Goodyear Tire & Rubber Company, 74
Google, 33
Grant, Andrew J. 118, 149
Gray, Carmel, 70
Great Depression, 1
Greater China, 47, 132
Gross Domestic Product (GDP), 18, 124, 149, 182
Guangzhou, 130, 183
Guthrie, Michelle, 48
Gyngell, David, 76

H

Harvard, 139
Harvard Business School Press, 93, 141
Hawker, Michael, 34
Healthcare Software, 42
Hearn, Lafcadio, 147
Heidrick & Struggles Asia Pacific, 4, 16, 28, 32, 33, 39, 60, 62, 64, 70, 72, 97, 107, 146, 149, 150, 155, 156, 163, 165
Hemstritch, Jane, 106
Hennin, Rob, 133
Herbold, Bob, 32
Hewlett–Packard (HP), 6
Heywood, Jamie, 133
High fliers, 98, 159
High potential, 76, 175
Hindustan Lever, 135, 136
Hold-outs, 124, 182
Honeywell, 125–126
Hong Kong, 14, 15, 22, 24, 45, 47, 48, 83, 95, 145, 150, 186
Hong Kong University of Science and Technology, 150
Huang Xingguo, 157
Huawei, 15
Human Resources (HR), 8, 35, 42, 57, 69, 73, 74, 78–80, 84, 107, 122, 130, 141, 142, 154, 169, 174
Hyderabad, 144
HyperCity, 140
HyperCity Retail, 141

I

IBM, 19, 22, 25, 45, 80, 83, 84, 151
IBM Consulting, 80, 84
IDS Logistics, 61
IMD International Search and Consulting, 136, 137
India Bazaar, 140
India Infoline, 17
Indian Institute of Technology, 13
Industrial, 14, 124, 147, 155, 162, 182, 187
Industry-based, 80
Information sharing, 58
Information Technology (IT), 17, 37, 104, 136
Infosys, 17, 21, 23, 26, 139
Infosys Leadership Institute, 136
Infosys Management Council, 136
ING, 77
Ingersoll–Rand, 124
INSEAD, 60, 63
Insurance, 34, 41, 133, 144, 162
Insurance Australia Group (IAG), 34
Intel Corporation, 143
Interim-to-permanent, 78, 80, 175
International Monetary Fund, 18
Internet, 33, 37, 39, 46, 95, 159
Internet Service Provider (ISP), 46
Intranet 58
IT and Information Technology Enabled Services (ITES), 136

J

Janssen–Cilag, 55, 57
Jiao Tong University, 150
John F. Welch Technology Center, 138
Johnson & Johnson Vision Care Asia Pacific, 61
Johnson, Brian, 35
Jones, David, 31
Jones Day, 158
Jones Lang LaSalle, 73
JP Morgan, 35
JP Morgan Partners, 88

INDEX

K
Kaizen, 7
Katz, Jeffrey, 103
Keane Inc., 79
Kella, Rob, 41
Kellogg School of Management, 91, 150
Ketzel, Mark, 95
Know-how, 16, 107
Kodak, 26
Koh Phee Wah, 56
Kotic, Bob, 77, 78, 80
KPMG, 94, 140, 141
Kraehe, Graham, 30, 31
Kraft, 73
Kumar, Pratik, 142, 143

L
Laker, Freddie, 56
Lam, James, 40
Lane, Ray, 33
Lark International, 16, 20, 26
Leadership, 1–5, 7–9, 18, 39, 46, 51–52, 57–58, 86–89, 99–101, 121–122, 124–128, 147, 150, 155–157, 161, 162, 165–167, 171–173, 186–187
Legal, 41, 46, 101, 170
Lenovo, 18, 19, 22, 25
Lesser, Eric, 84, 85
Leung, Antony, 47
Levermore, Andrew, 141
Lewis, Kenneth, 86
Liebelt, Graeme, 23, 24, 26
Life cycle, 57
Lingua franca, 137
Long term, 21, 28, 31, 39, 40, 49, 73, 90–92, 122, 126, 128, 130–132, 142, 143, 157, 160, 161, 167, 184, 185
LookSmart, 159
Los Angeles Times, 153
Low-cost, 59, 73, 123, 124, 182, 184
Lucknow, 139
Lumley Children's Cancer Institute Australia, 163
Lyon, Mark, 161

M
Ma, Mary, 19, 22, 25, 26
MacDonald, Randy, 84
Macroeconomic, 16
Mahler, Peter, 54, 104, 105
Mallesons, Stephen Jaques, 47
Mandarin, 24, 60
Maoist-style, 14
Marathe, Ajay, 144
Marketing-oriented, 21
Marshall, Darren, 39
Maslow's, 3
Mazumdar-Show, Kiran, 139
MBA, 57, 60, 129, 150, 183
MBF Australia, 70
McGuire, Eddie, 76
McKerihan, Steve, 159
McKinsey and Co., 18, 118, 149, 159
McKinsey Global Institute, 152
Media, 30, 33, 39, 46, 51, 56, 105, 107, 134, 154
Media Development Authority, 107
Medium-sized, 25
Megalopolis, 154
Metro, 140
Microsoft, 32, 144
Middle East, 17
Middle Kingdom, 14
Middle-management, 126
Miles, Stephen, 32, 33
Mind-set, 9, 23, 27, 121, 136, 144, 153, 162, 186
Mission-critical, 126
MIT, 150
Mitchell, Pat, 87
Monsanto, 94
Monster, 37
More, 141
Morison, Bob, 93
Morrant, Vic, 80
Motorola, 158
Mulcahy, John, 70
Multimillion-dollar, 159
Multiple Sclerosis Limited, 160
Multi-strategy, 69
Mumbai, 17
Murdoch, Rupert, 32
Murnane, Paul, 160, 161
Murthy, N.R. Narayana, 13, 14, 137

N
Nagesh, B.S., 140
Nair, Rajiv, 144
National Australia Bank, 30, 44, 79, 105
Nelson, Phil, 133
New Delhi, 13, 158
New York, 26, 32, 153
News Corporation, 32
Newsweek, 151
Next-generation, 38, 155, 169
Ng Yoke Weng, 64
Nicol, Edward, 53, 54
Nilekani, Nandan, 18, 21, 23, 25
Nine Network, 76, 77
Non-executive, 160
Nonprofit, 155, 159–163
Nortel, 45
Northern Hemisphere, 94
Northwestern University, 91, 150
Novartis Pharmaceuticals, 128

O
Oberoi, 135
Offshoring, 15, 139
Offshore, 15, 17, 20–22, 46, 83, 85, 94, 95, 138, 167
On-boarding, 31, 61–65, 74, 82, 104, 123, 135, 168, 173, 175
Open-mindedness, 18
Oracle, 33
Orbitz, 103
Organization of Petroleum Exporting Countries (OPEC), 16
Orica, 16, 22, 24, 26
Original Equipment Manufacturing (OEM), 15
Orwellian, 47

P
Packer, Kerry, 33, 76
Page, Larry, 33
Partner, 33, 168
Part-time, 79, 175

INDEX

Paterson, John, 45
Pearl River Delta, 14
People 27, 28, 30, 31, 41, 42, 53, 54, 61, 82, 85, 88, 104, 105, 180
PepsiCo, 139, 159
Performance, 4, 6, 33, 63, 86, 87, 90, 102, 104–105, 119, 129, 179, 183
Photo finish, 31, 168
Photon Infotech, 133
Polistuk, Eugene V., 102
Post-Boomers, 92
Post–World War II, 7, 15
Pottruck, David S., 89
Power-hungry, 51
Price, Don, 144
Princeton University, 13
Private, 47, 48, 145, 159, 170–171
Private Equity (PE), 47–49, 159, 170–171
Procter & Gamble, 73
Product-driven, 25
Professional Development, 37, 141
Professional Service Firms (PSFs), 141–143, 185
Professional Services, 87, 141
Profit and Loss (P&L), 37
Providence Equity Partners, 48
Prudential, 70
Public Broadcasting System, 87
Publishing and Broadcasting Limited, 33
Purpose-built, 4

Q

Qantas Airways, 41
Quick fix, 8, 130, 131, 184
Quick-action-oriented, 145

R

Radius, 80
Railcorp, 71
Ranbaxy, 138
Rao, Baru, 144
Reagan, Ronald, 13
Record-breaking, 149
Recruiting, 75, 137, 182
Relationship-building, 84
Reliance Fresh, 140
Reliance Industries, 135
Reliance Mart, 140
Research and Development (R&D), 37, 40, 138, 139, 185
Return-to-India (R2I), 145–146, 186
Reuters, 139
Richard, Goyder, 30
Richardson, Dave, 52
Roberts, Chris, 24, 26, 27
Roll, Martin, 38
Ross, James, 80
Royal Blind Society, 162
RSM & Co., 143
Résumés, 37, 55, 59, 144

S

Sales-oriented, 21
Salgame, Rangu, 144
Salt, Bernard, 94
Saltuk, Ertop, 133
Sano, Tadakatsu, 158
Sanofi-Aventis, 129
Sarbanes-Oxley, 40, 170
Savage, Bob, 3
Sawhney, Mohanbir, 90
Schmidt, Eric, 33
Schwab, Charles, 89
Sealord, 16
Second-in-command, 32
Second-tier, 126
Senge, Peter, 104
Shake up, 26
Shakeout, 140
Shanghai, China, 26, 119, 130, 133, 150, 183
Shanta Biotech, 139
Shelf life, 57
Shenzhen, 14, 15, 45, 148, 166
Shenzhen Watch and Clock Association, 14
Shi Zhengrong, 158
Shoehorned, 118
Shoppers' Stop, 140
Shoprite, 140
Short term, 77, 79, 142, 145, 160, 162, 175, 184–186
Shortsighted, 90
Siemens, 124
Siewert, Patrick, 48, 49
Sign-on, 17, 78
Silicon Valley, 144
Singapore, 22, 37, 38, 45, 47, 52, 60, 75, 76, 83, 107, 145, 155, 158, 186
Singapore Airlines, 52
Singapore Media Authority, 107
SingTel Group, 64
SinoCast China Business Daily, 14
Six Sigma, 4
Skill sets, 8, 17, 137, 162
Smith, Frederick W., 88, 109
Social Ventures Australia, 159
Sociodemographic, 150
Soviet Union, 13, 95
Spencer's, 140, 141
St. George Bank, 159
Stanford University, 19
Star India Bazaar, 140
STAR Television, 48
Start-up, 33, 159
Steelmaker, 18
Stephens, Mary-Anne, 162, 163
Stopgap, 135
Straightforward, 23, 108
Strategic Leaders Program, 136
Subprime, 1, 139
Sugar, Alan, 65
Sullivan, Belinda, 162
Sun Pharma, 138
Sun Tzu, 4
Suncorp, 70
Suntech, 158
Supply chain, 73, 74, 102, 104, 105, 135, 140, 144, 185
Sydney, 41, 71, 77, 148, 159, 161
Sydney Water, 71

T

Tata AIG Life Insurance, 133
Tata Consultancy Services, 139

Tata Group, 136
Tata, Noel, 140
Team-building, 58
Technology, 13, 15, 25, 32, 42, 44, 53, 71, 84, 85, 104, 105, 107, 117, 128, 133, 136–138, 141, 143, 144, 150, 168, 183
Tech-savvy, 152
Tedjarati, Shane, 125
Tenix, 33
Tesco, 140
Testa, Emilio Paolo, 93
Texas Instruments (TI), 138
Texas Pacific Group, 19
The Wall Street Journal, 13, 14, 39, 41, 45
Thomas, Ian Q.R., 134
Thompson, Michael, 64
Thornley, Evan, 159
Thornton, Grant, 136
Thornton, Helen, 41
Three Gorges dam, 124
Tianjin, 6, 156, 157
Tianjin Municipal People's Government, 157
Tight-knit, 152
Top management teams, 137
Topfer, Mort, 33
Top-performing, 88
Toshiba, 56
Trade-off, 158
Traditionalist, 92
Traill, Michael, 159
Transcultural, 15
Transgenerational, 15
Tredenick, Michelle, 44, 105
Trent, 140
Tsao, Jim, 48
Tso, David, 20

U

U2, 160
Uber-investor, 3
UBS banking research, 34
Ultracompetitive, 153
Uniken, Tina, 144
Unilever, 73, 136, 139
United States (US), 1, 13, 17, 18, 22, 35, 37, 44, 45, 62, 81, 82, 87, 93, 118, 124, 138–140, 151, 169, 170, 182
University of Sydney, 77
University of Technology, 16
Upward, 151

V

Vacancy, 69
Vaneris, Bessie, 79
Venardos, George, 34
VentureRepubic, 38
Videoconferencing, 85
Viewpoint, 83, 87, 101, 179
Vinci, Donna, 44
Virgin Atlantic, 56
Virgin Mobile India, 133
Vision Australia, 162
Vitasoy, 16, 22, 24
Vodafone Essar, 133

W

Wadhwa, Ashok, 142
Wall Street, 1, 15
Wal-Mart Stores, 135, 140
Washington University, 150
Watkins, Michael, 63
Welch, Jack, 3, 7, 99, 181
Wesfarmers, 30
West 7, 15, 44, 57, 59, 81, 145, 154
Western, 13, 17, 18, 19, 22, 25, 26, 27, 28, 57, 59, 86, 105, 124, 131, 137, 139, 147, 152, 154, 157, 187
Western International Communications, 105
Westpac, 43, 53
Wilhelm, Marcus, 133
Williams, Boyd, 73
Wipro, 136, 139, 142, 143
Woods, Tiger, 99
Working-age, 17
World War II, 1, 7, 14, 15
World-changing, 14
World-class, 5, 75, 76, 134
World-leading, 149
Wuhan, 130, 183

X

X factors, 124

Y

Yahoo, 95
Yomiuri Shimbun, 39

Z

Zakaria, Fareed, 151
Zerbib Sandrine, 132
ZTE Corporation, 15